Spelling & Grammar

Daily Practice Workbook
20 weeks of fun activities

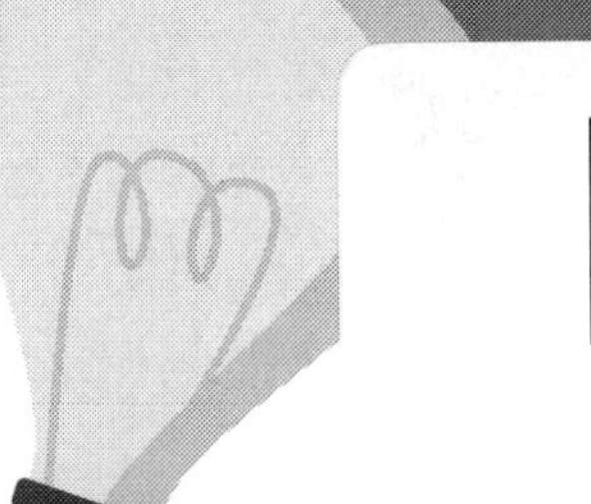

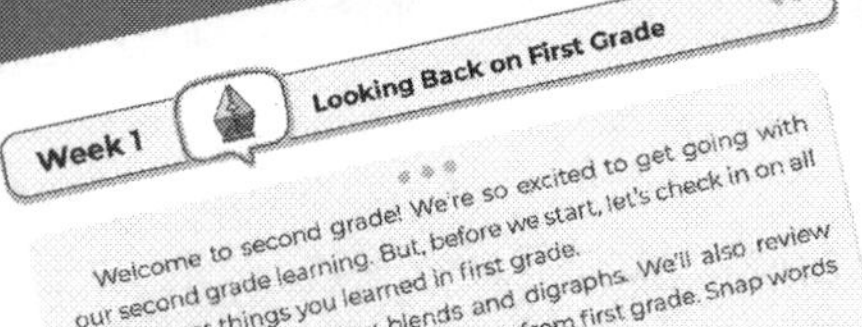

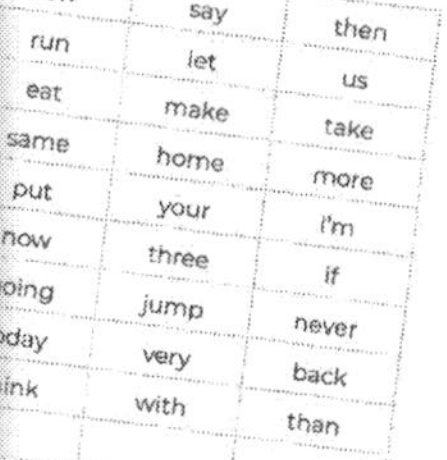

ArgoPrep is one of the leading providers of supplemental educational products and services. We offer affordable and effective test prep solutions to educators, parents and students. Learning should be fun and easy! To access more resources visit us at www.argoprep.com.

Our goal is to make your life easier, so let us know how we can help you by e-mailing us at: info@argoprep.com.

- ArgoPrep is a recipient of the prestigious **Mom's Choice Award.**

- ArgoPrep also received the 2019 **Seal of Approval** from Homeschool.com for our award-winning workbooks.

- ArgoPrep was awarded the 2019 **National Parenting Products Award, Gold Medal Parent's Choice Award** and **the Tillywig Brain Child Award.**

Table of Contents

Week	Topic	Snap Words	Standard
1	First Grade Review: Blends, Digraphs and Snap Word Review	his, said, saw, say, then, they, but, let run, us, yes, big, eat, make, take, have, came, same, home, more, not, of, put, your, I'm, into, little, now, three, if, or, read, going, jump, never, there, any, today, very, back, best, just, think, with, than, that	1RF1a, 1RF3a,1RF3b 1RF3c, 1RF3d, 1RF3e
2	First Grade Review: Vowel Teams, R-Controlled Vowels and Snap Word Review	was, could, from, mother, should, would, don't, away, each, easy, wait, last, near, need, next, been, about, down, house, our, know, school, much, such, two, who, few, because, high, might, over, their, under, want, were, family, find, kind, ask, them, things, walk, everyone, everything, myself, after, always, soon, enough, great, idea, often, pretty, until	1RF1a, 1RF3a,1RF3b 1RF3c, 1RF3d, 1RF3e
3	Homophones	eight, ate, see, sea, eye, I, hear, here	2RF3a, 2RF3b, 2RF3c, 2RF3e
4	Contractions	two, too, to, your, you're, there, their, they're	2.ELAL.24.h
5	Common, Proper, and Possessive Nouns	school, people, cousin, was, could	2.ELAL.24.c, 2.ELAL.25.h
6	Plural Nouns	better, follow, happen, different, very	2.ELAL.24.e, 2.ELAL.24.f, 2.ELAL.24.g
7	Compound Words	somewhere, anyone, nobody, outside	2.ELAL.24.d, 2.ELAL.26.d
8	Root Words, Prefixes, and Suffixes	question, slowly, suddenly, probably, usually	2.ELAL.26.b, 2.ELAL.26.c
9	Verb Agreement: Make it Make Sense!	answer, goes, does, begin, trouble	2.ELAL.24.g, 2.ELAL.24.l

10	Adjectives and Adverbs	special, great, excited, beautiful, old	2.ELAL.24.m, 2.ELAL.27.b, 2.ELAL.27.c, 2.ELAL.27.d
11	Review week - writing, reading, and correcting sentences with homophones, contractions, nouns, verbs, adjectives, and adverbs		2RF3, 2.ELA.24, 2.ELA.25, 2.ELA.26, 2.ELA.27
12	Interrogatives	when, went, what, where	2.ELAL.24.h
13	Prepositions	together, several, begin, befor	2.ELAL.24.i
14	Pronouns	themselves, either, while, everybody	2.ELAL.24.k
15	Commas	enough, again, being, ready	2.ELAL.25.g
16	Conjunctions	sometimes, understand, with, against	2.ELAL.24.n
17	Simple and Compound Sentences	terrible, through, excited	2.ELAL.24.o
18	Collective Nouns	everything, about, bare, bear	2.ELAL.24.d
19	Proofreading and Spelling Strategies	Great, favorite, maybe	2.ELAL.25.b, 2.ELAL.25.d, 2.ELAL.25.e, 2.ELAL.25.f
20	Review week - writing, reading, and correcting sentences with homophones, contractions, nouns, verbs, adjectives, adverbs, interrogatives, prepositions, pronouns, commas, conjunctions, simple and compound sentences, and collective nouns		1RF1a, 1RF3a,1RF3b 1RF3c, 1RF3d, 1RF3e

Table of Contents

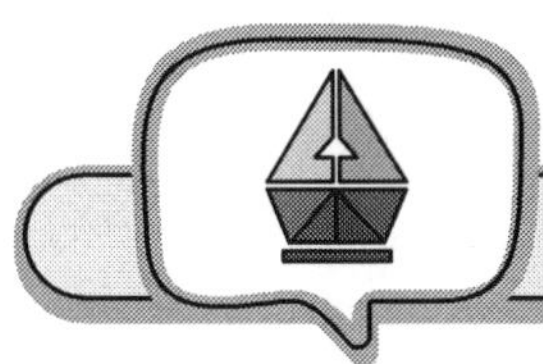

How to Use this Book

Welcome to our 2nd Grade Spelling & Grammar Workbook, a cornerstone in supporting your child's critical phase of literacy development. This comprehensive workbook, curated to meet the demands of the English Language Arts Standards, particularly emphasizes the Foundational Reading Standard Skills.

A Closer Look:

Week-by-Week Learning: Dive into 20 weeks of structured content. Each week introduces a pivotal topic, supplemented with varied exercises and activities, promoting in-depth learning and practice.

The Significance of 2nd Grade: At this stage, students experience transformative growth in their literacy capabilities. Our workbook facilitates this journey by introducing words students must know for their grade level. This workbook covers homophones, contractions, possessive nouns, plural nouns, compound words, prefix, suffix, verbs, adjectives, adverbs, interrogatives, prepositions, pronouns, commas, conjunctions, collective nouns and more.

Aligning with Standards: With our workbook, you're not just investing in a practice book; you're choosing a resource meticulously crafted to mirror the standards. This ensures that each topic, exercise, and activity pushes your child closer to mastery. This workbook is 100% state-aligned with 2nd Grade Foundational Reading Standards.

Enrich the Experience: For those aiming to augment reading comprehension, we recommend our Common Core ELA (English Language Arts) workbook series.

Video Support: This workbook comes included with detailed video explanations taught by a licenced teacher on our website. We highly recommend watching the accompanying videos as they will emphasize key spelling and grammar principles. Video explanations to your workbook are free.

How to access video explanations?

Go to **argoprep.com/spelling2**
OR scan the QR Code:

First Grade Review: Blends, Digraphs and Snap Word Review

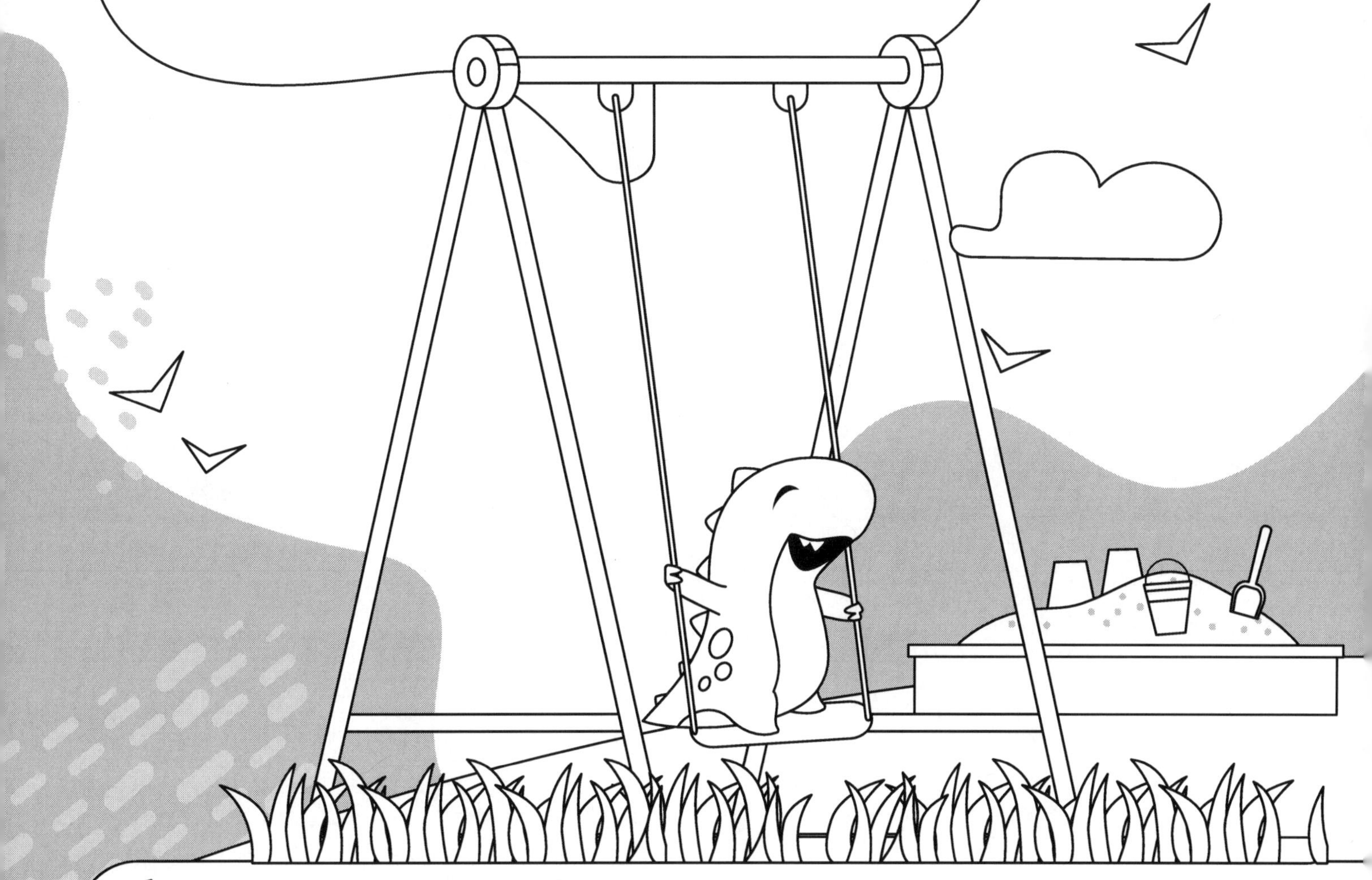

This week, you'll review some important reading and writing concepts from first grade.

Welcome to second grade! We're so excited to get going with our second grade learning. But, before we start, let's check in on all of the great things you learned in first grade.

This week, we'll review blends and digraphs. We'll also review some snap words you may remember from first grade. Snap words are words you should know in a snap!

With your adult, review the charts below.

Blends

bl	cl	fl	gl
pl	sl	br	cr
dr	fr	gr	pr

tr	sk	sm	sn

sp	st	sw	

sh	ch	th	wh

In the activities on the next few pages, you will practice reading and writing words with blends and digraphs.

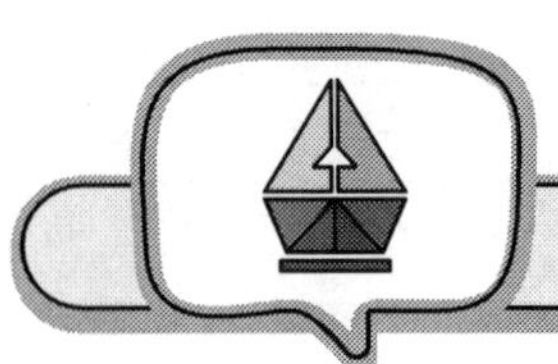

Reading and Spelling Words with Blends

Directions: Look at the pictures below and **write** the blend you hear. Some blends may be used more than once.

Blend Word Bank: pr, sw, sp, st, cl, cr, sk, pl, dr, tr, fr

 __omp	 __unk	 __ane	 __own	 __airs
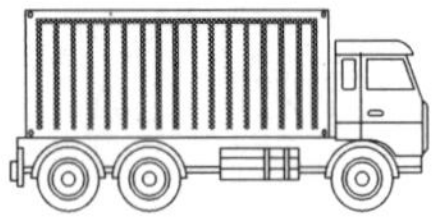 __uck	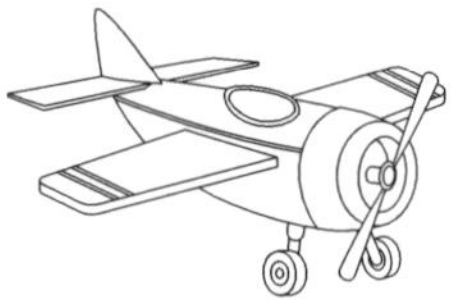 __ane	 __uit	 __esent	 wa__
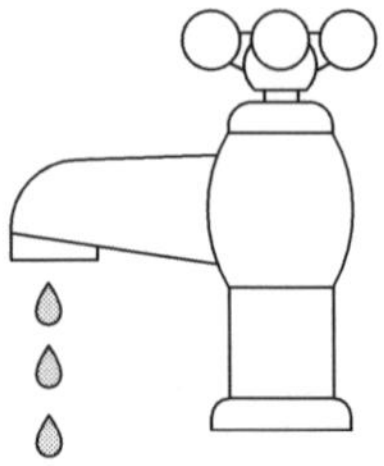 __ip	 __eater			

Read the words below.

blend	crop	snap	plum
pram	slip	brim	cramp
drum	swim	stop	flag

Now, **write** the 12 words below. The first one has been completed for you.

blend		

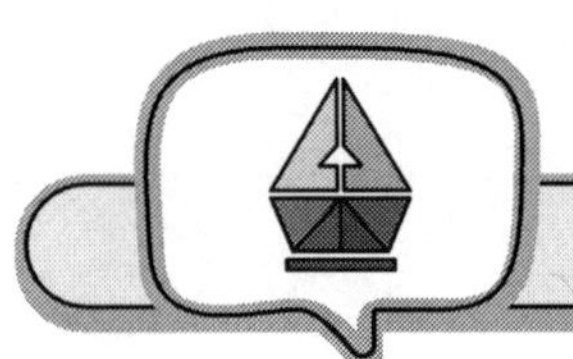 

Reading and Spelling Words with Digraphs

You may remember from first grade that digraphs are two letters that make a brand new sound.

Directions: Look at the pictures below and **write** the digraph you hear. The digraphs will be used more than once.

Digraph Word Bank: ch, sh, th

___umb	___ip	___ark	___air
___ild	___eep	___in	___ur___
___oe	ba___tub	___eese	___op

Read the words below.

with	much	what	math
than	shell	church	thing
such	crutch	think	where

Now, **write** the 12 words below. The first one has been completed for you.

with		

Writing a Story with Blends and Digraphs

Directions: Read the list of blends and digraphs below. Then, use at least three of the words to **write** a story. Be sure to use correct capitalization and punctuation! Afterwards, draw a picture to match your story.

Word Bank

clap	drum	stomp	sheep
cheese	fish	wheel	thorn
fly	thunder	plane	storm

Snap Word Practice

Directions: Read the list of your first grade snap words below. If you don't know a word, **circle it**! That way you'll know which words you need to practice.

his	said	saw	say	then
they	but	run	let	us
yes	big	eat	make	take
have	came	same	home	more
not	of	put	your	I'm
into	little	now	three	if
or	read	going	jump	never
there	any	today	very	back
best	just	think	with	than
that				

Look at the words you circled. If you knew all the words, great job! Pick three words that were harder for you. In the activity below, we will play a game called **Timed Write**.

Directions: To play this game, start a timer for one minute. Write your word as many times as you can in a minute. Then, see if you can beat your time!

Word Choice 1: ....

Word Choice 2: ....

Word Choice 3: ....

First Grade Review: Vowel Teams, R-Controlled Vowels and Snap Word Review

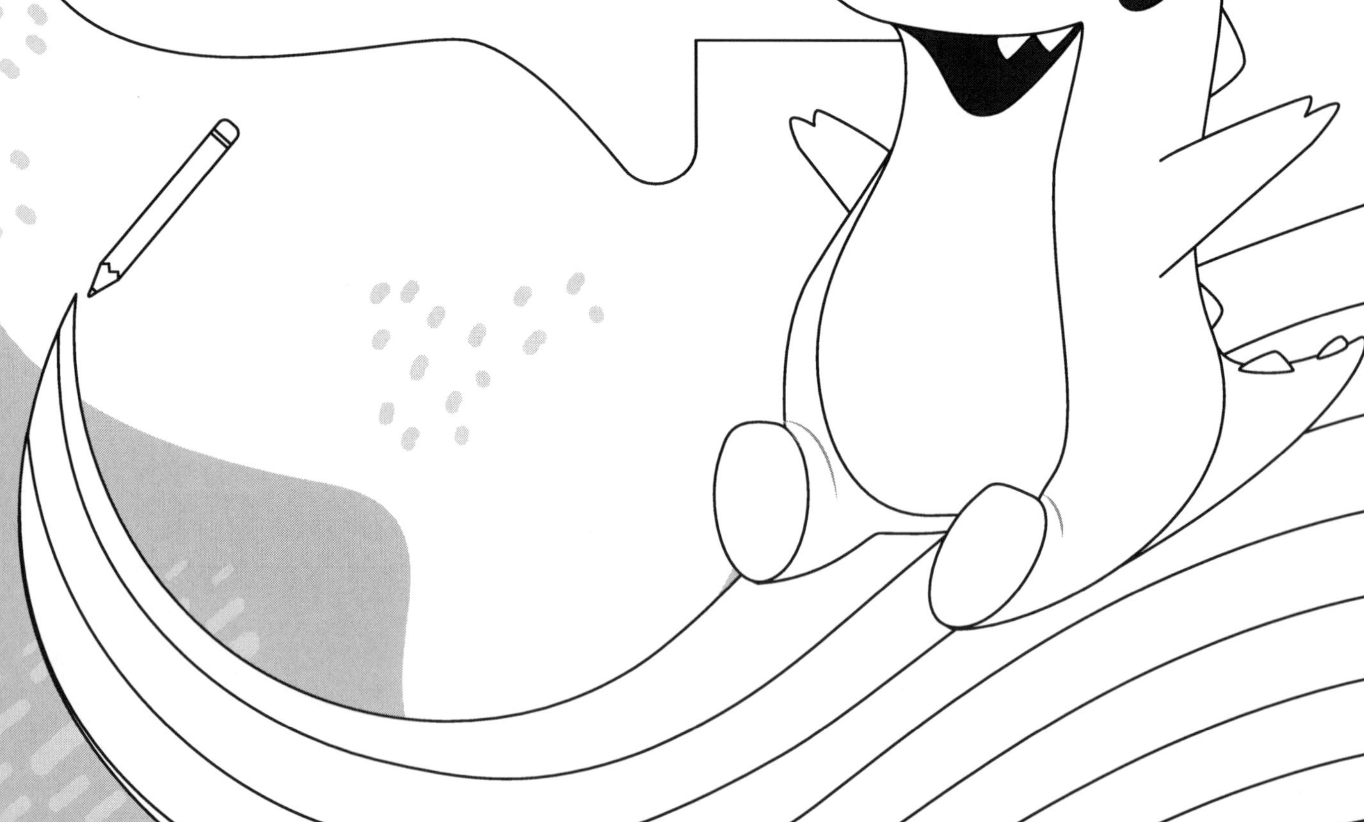

This week, you'll spend a little bit more time reviewing important first grade concepts before you get into second grade learning next week.

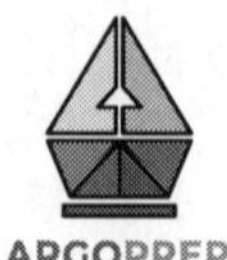

Last week, you reviewed the blends and digraphs you learned in first grade along with some snap words.

This week, we'll review vowel teams and r-controlled vowels. We'll also review the rest of the snap words you may remember from first grade. Remember, snap words are words you should know in a snap!

With your adult, review the charts below.

Vowel Teams

Rain	Play	Neigh	Pause
ai	ay	eigh	au
Paw	Fruit	Light	Seal
aw	ui	igh	ea
Bee	Stew	Bread	Mouth
ee	ew	ea	ou

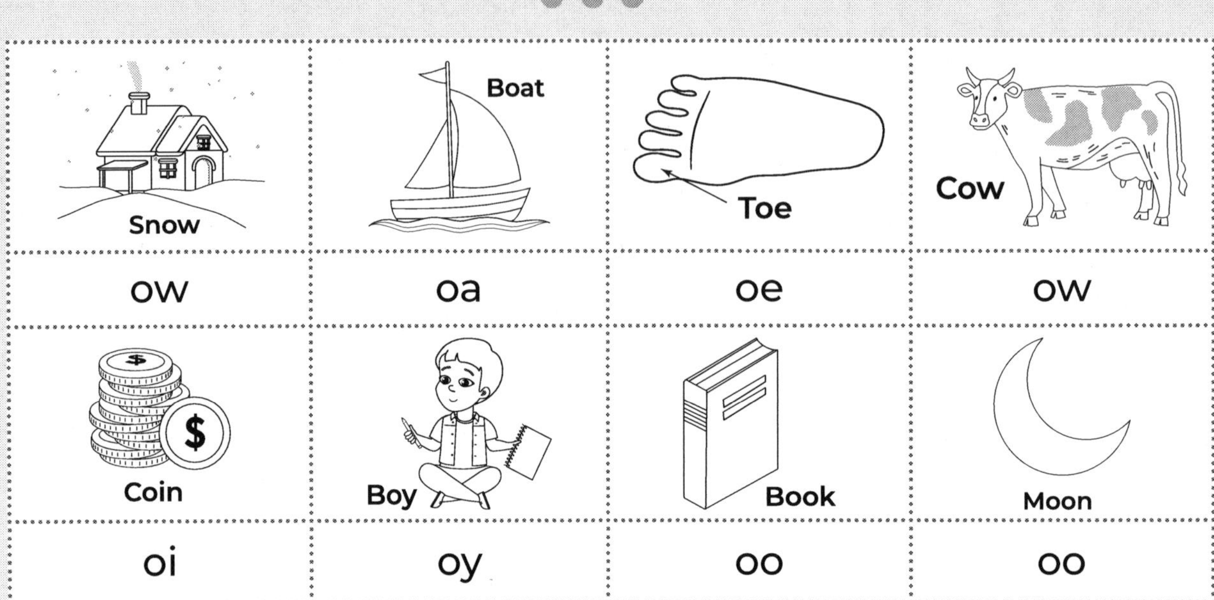

R-Controlled Vowels

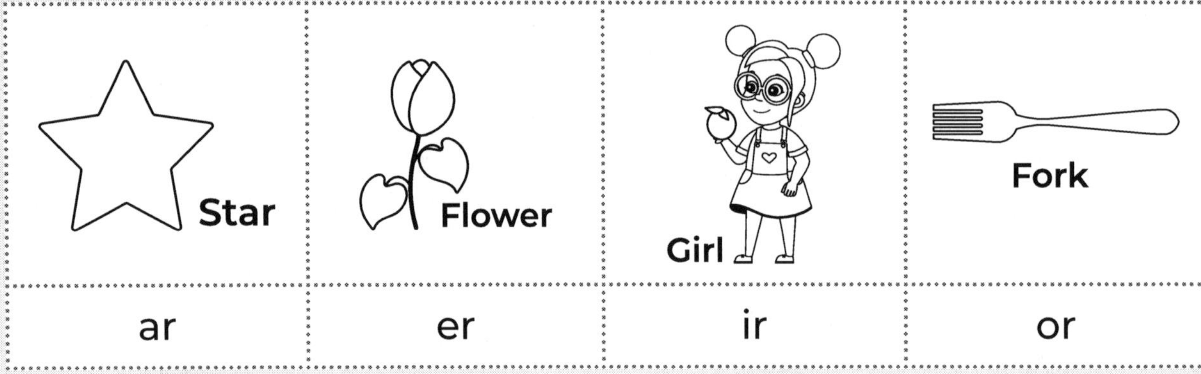

In the activities on the next few pages, you will practice reading and writing words with vowel teams and r-controlled vowels.

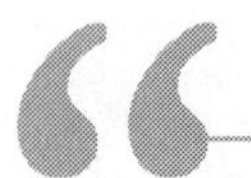

Reading and Spelling Words with Vowel Teams

You may remember from first grade that vowel teams are two vowels that make one sound. Sometimes, vowel teams make the sound of the first vowel in the team, and sometimes, vowel teams make a brand new sound.

Directions: Look at the pictures below and **write** the vowel team you hear. Some vowel teams may be used more than once. Remember that some vowel teams make the same sound, so double check your spelling to see if the word you wrote looks right!

Word Bank: igh, ai, oo, oi, oa, ea, ee, aw, ay, ou

pl＿＿	l＿＿t	b＿＿k
s＿＿＿	br＿＿d	m＿＿th

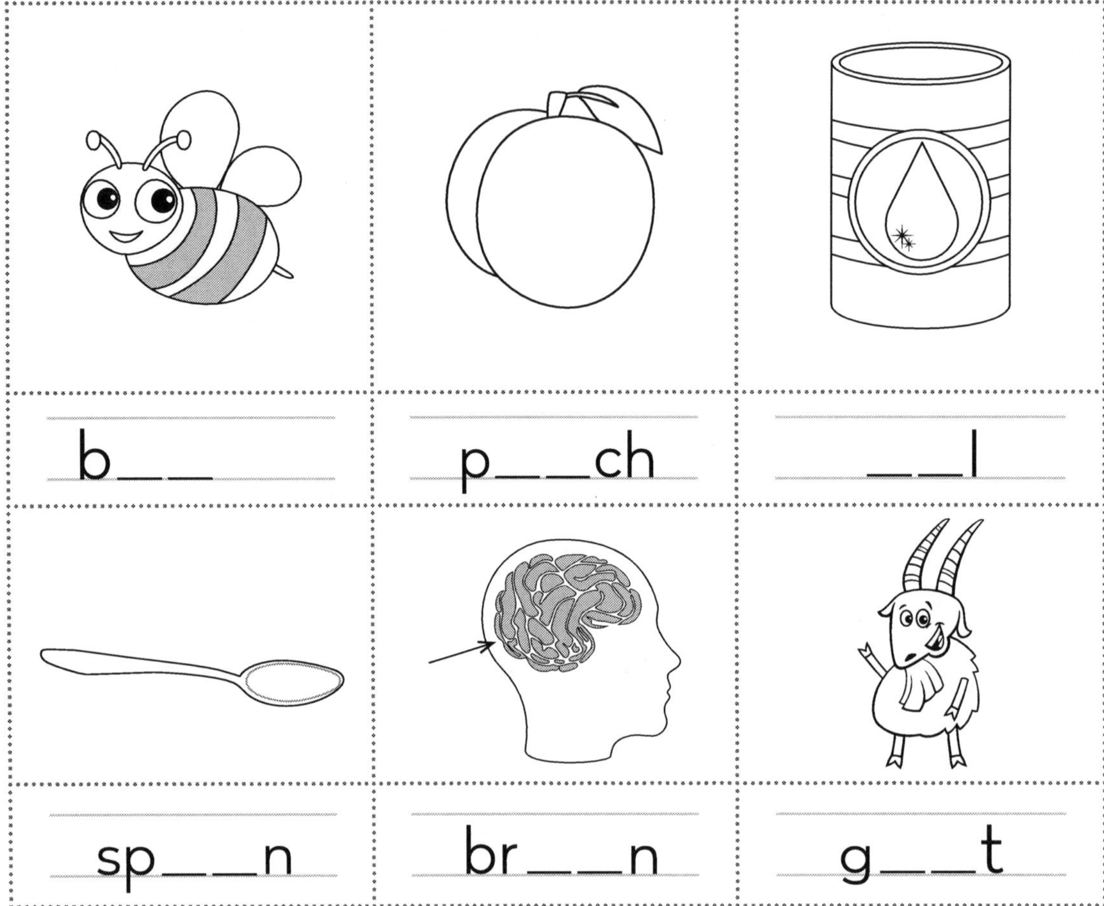

Read the words below.

snail	bear	eight	foil
moat	cow	instead	fright
crew	soybean	dream	crawl

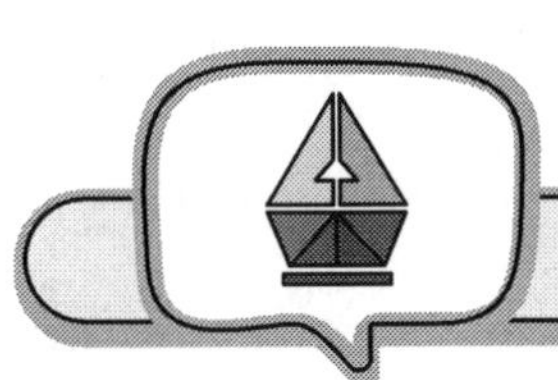

Now, **write** the 12 words below. The first one has been completed for you.

snail		

Reading and Spelling Words with R-controlled Vowels

You may remember from first grade that r-controlled vowels are vowels that change sounds when there is an r after them.

R-controlled vowels can be tricky to write. ER, IR, and UR all make the same sound, so it can be hard to tell which r-controlled vowel to pick! ER usually comes at the end of a word, but IR and UR usually come in the middle of a word.

Directions: Look at the pictures below and **write** the r-controlled vowel you hear. The r- controlled vowel will be used more than once. Double check your spelling to be sure the words look right!

R-Controlled Vowel Word Bank: ar, er, ir, or, ur

sh___t   st___   c___tain

wat___

n___se

guit___

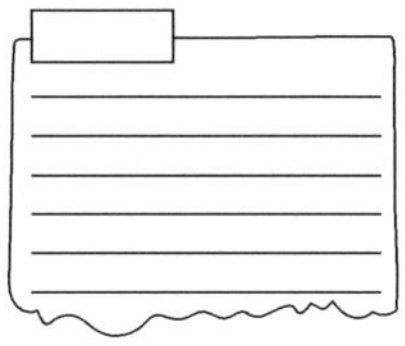

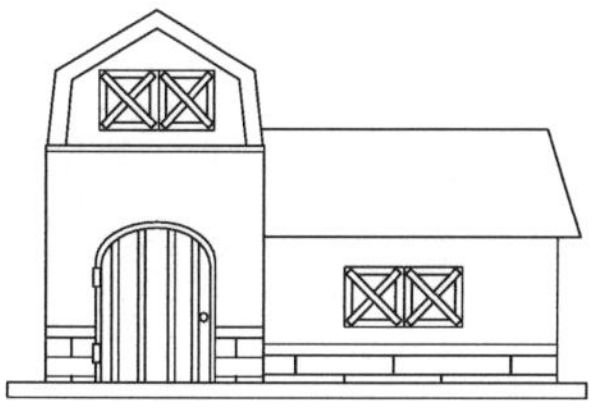

c___n

pap___

b___n

doct___

flow___

b___d

Read the words below.

first	Carl	third	purse
burst	hammer	burn	shark
fern	birthday	March	shower

Now, **write** the 12 words below. The first one has been completed for you.

first		

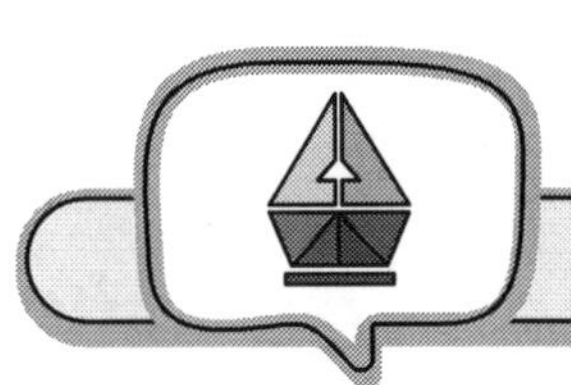

Reading a Story with Vowel Teams and R-Controlled Vowels

Directions: Read the story below. When you are done, you will answer some questions about the story, so pay attention!

Carl and Ashlee went to the store to get some fruit. They were going to make a fruit salad! Ashlee wanted some peaches, but Carl said he liked strawberries better. They got both.

At home, Ashlee read the cookbook and Carl chopped the fruit. Carl added juice and some sugar to the bowl. Then, the fruit salad was done!

Ashlee put the salad in the blue bowls, and Carl set the table with forks. Carl said, "This is so good!"

1. What fruit did Carl and Ashlee put in the salad?

   A. Apples

   B. Bananas

   C. Peaches

2. What did Ashlee do while Carl chopped fruit?

   A. Went to the store

   B. Read a cookbook

   C. Washed the dishes

3. What did Ashlee and Carl eat their fruit salad with?

    A. Forks

    B. Spoons

    C. Their hands

Draw a picture of the fruits in the fruit salad.

Snap Word Practice

Directions: Read the list of your first grade snap words below. If you don't know a word, **circle it**! That way you'll know which words you need to practice.

was	could	from	mother	should
would	don't	away	each	easy
wait	last	near	need	next
been	about	down	house	our
know	school	much	such	two
who	few	because	high	might
over	their	under	want	were
family	find	kind	ask	them
things	walk			

Look at the words you circled. If you knew all the words, great job! Pick **three words** that were harder for you. In the activity below, we will play a game called **Pyramid Write**.

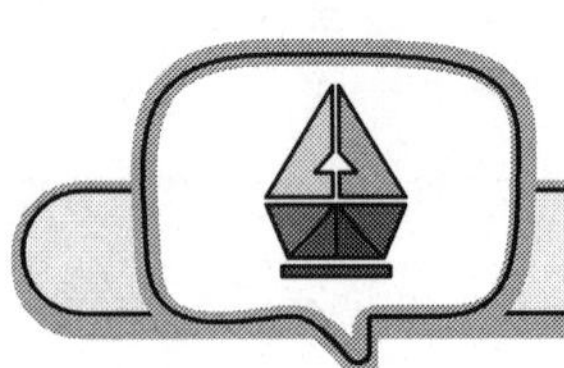

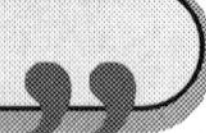

Directions: To play this game, you will write the three words one letter at a time, making a pyramid shape!

Example: went

w
we
wen
went

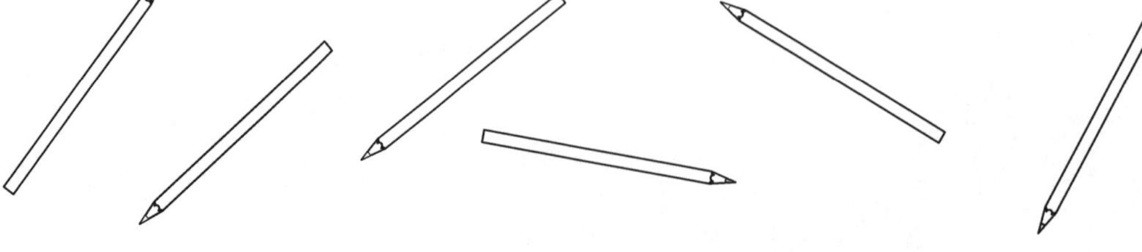

Homophones

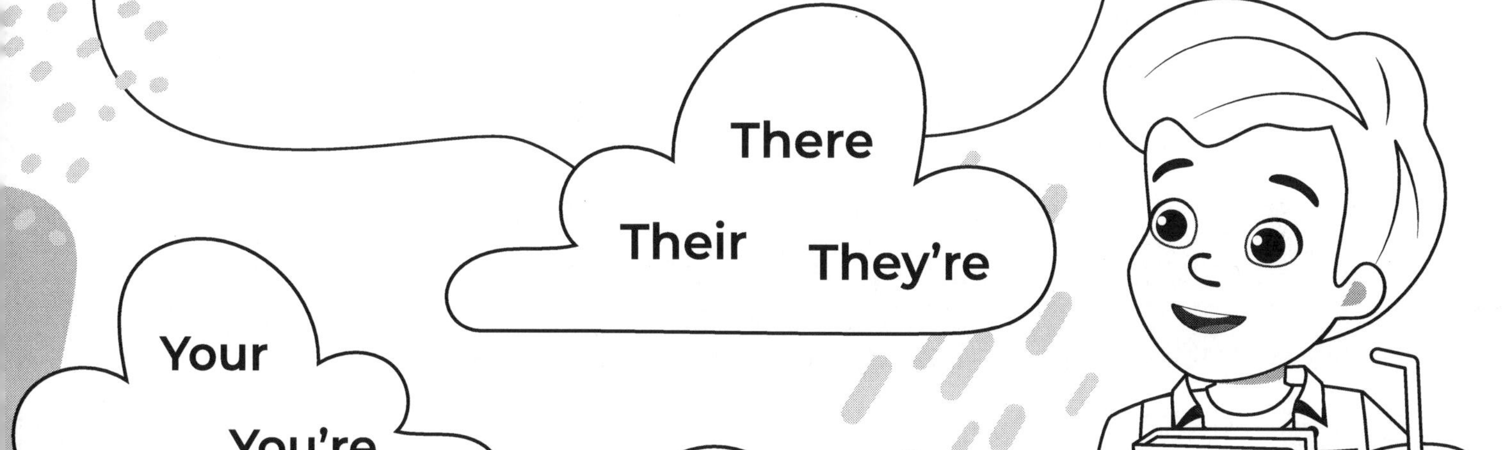

Welcome to your first week of second grade learning! This week, you'll learn about homophones, which are a special type of word.

Last week, you finished up your first grade review, so now it is time to get to your second grade learning!

This week, we'll learn about homophones. **Homophones** are words that sound the same but mean different things! They can trip you up when you're reading and writing.

With your adult, **read** the list of common homophones below.

to - used for direction (e.g., "I'm going to the store.")
too - meaning also or very (e.g., "I want to go, too.")
two - the number 2 (e.g., "I have two apples.")

there - indicating a place (e.g., "The park is over there.")
their - showing possession (e.g., "It's their ball.")
they're - contraction of "they are" (e.g., "They're coming to the party.")

your - showing possession (e.g., "Is this your book?")
you're - contraction of "you are" (e.g., "You're my best friend.")

its - showing possession by "it" (e.g., "The dog wagged its tail.")
it's - contraction of "it is" (e.g., "It's a sunny day.")

bare - uncovered or naked (e.g., "The tree was bare in winter.")
bear - a large mammal (e.g., "The bear lives in the forest.")

no - indicating the absence or negation (e.g., "No, thank you.")
know - to be aware or have information about something (e.g., "I know the answer.")

ate - past tense of "eat" (e.g., "She ate lunch.")
eight - the number 8 (e.g., "There are eight crayons.")

here - indicating a place (e.g., "Come here, please.")
hear - to perceive sound with your ears (e.g., "I can hear the music.")

one - the number 1 (e.g., "I have one toy.")
won - past tense of "win" (e.g., "He won the game.")

write - to put words on paper (e.g., "I can write my name.")
right - the opposite of left (e.g., "Turn right at the corner.")

our - showing possession by "we" (e.g., "This is our house.")
hour - a unit of time (e.g., "An hour has 60 minutes.")

son - a male child (e.g., "He is my son.")
sun - the star that provides light and heat to Earth (e.g., "The sun is shining.")

In the activities on the next few pages, you will practice reading and writing homophones.

Homophone Hunt

For this activity, you will need a book, magazine, or newspaper.

Directions: Hunt for homophones in your book, magazine, or newspaper. When you find a homophone, **write** the sentence it is in on the line and **underline** the homophone.

Homophone Examples

to	there	your	its	here
bear	no	are	one	write
our	son	too	their	you're
it's	hear	bare	know	eight
won	right	hour	sun	two
they're				

Example: I like <u>to</u> go <u>to</u> the store.

1. ____

2. ____

3. ____

4. ____

5. ____

There, Their, and They're

One set of homophones you'll see often is there, their, and they're. Even though they all sound the same, they have different meanings!

One way you can remember these homophones is with pictures.

(show ownership)
That is **their** <u>toy</u>.

(refers to a place)
The ball is over **there**.

(a contraction for they are)
They're going to the park.

Write a sentence with each homophone. **Draw** a picture to match your sentence.

there

their

they're

You're and Your

Another common pair of homophones you will see is you're and your.

You're is a contraction (you'll learn more about those later in this workbook!). It means "you are."

Your is a word used to show possession.

You can remember these homophones with pictures, too!

(show ownership)
Here is **your** toy.

TIP - can you replace **your** with **my** ?

eg. **Your** house is big ⟶ **My** house is big

(a contraction for you are)
You're a great friend.

TIP - can you replace **you're** with **you are** ?

eg. **You're** funny ⟶ **You are** funny

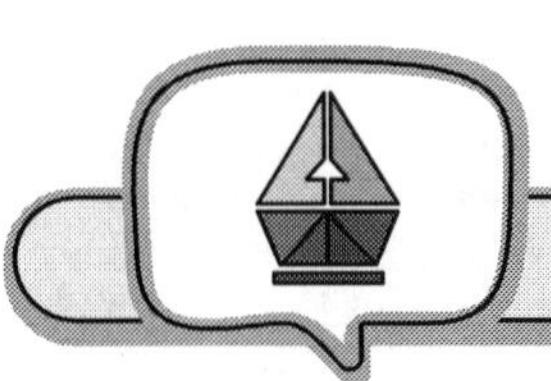

Write a sentence with each homophone. **Draw** a picture to match your sentence.

your

you're

Too, To, and Two

The last set of homophones we'll talk about today is too, to, and two.

Too means "also."

To means someone is going in a direction.

Two is a number.

Just like the homophones from activities 2 and 3, some pictures can help you remember when to use these!

(two) the number 2
I had <u>two</u> tacos at dinner.

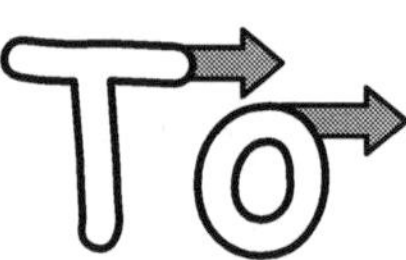

in the direction of
I walked <u>to</u> school.

also or in excess
I ate <u>too</u> much ice cream.

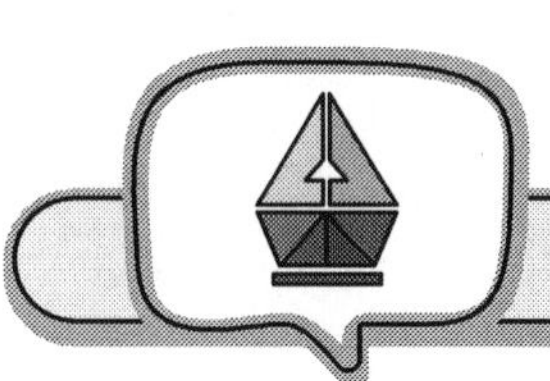 

Write a sentence with each homophone. **Draw** a picture to match your sentence.

too

to

two

Homophone Quiz

Directions: Read the sentences. Then, circle the correct homophone for the blank.

1. I am going .... school.

   A. to

   B. too

   C. two

2. .... dog is cute.

   A. They're

   B. There

   C. Their

3. How is .... mother?

   A. your

   B. you're

4. .... funny!

   A. Your

   B. You're

5. Can we go .... this weekend?

   A. they're

   B. there

   C. their

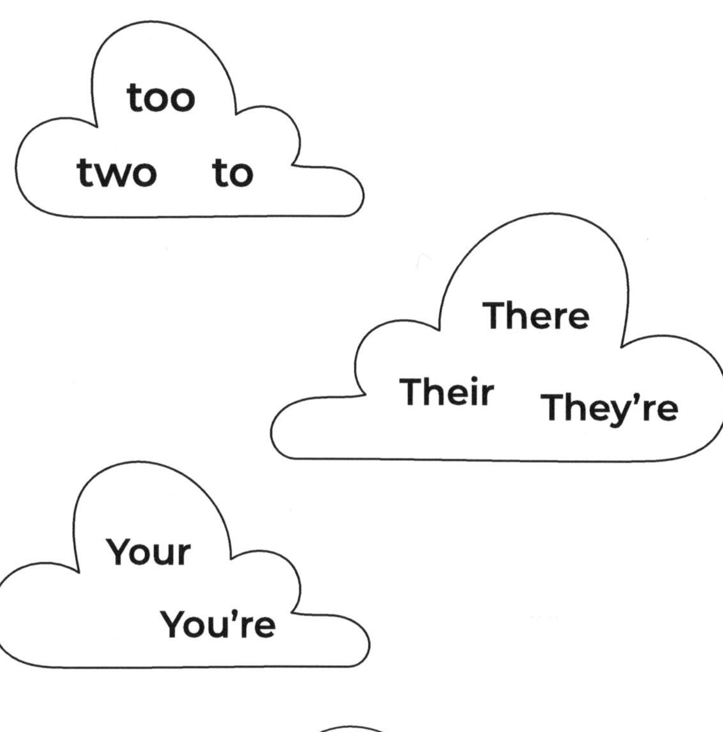

Snap Word Practice

Today we will learn **eight** new snap words! With your adult, read the snap words below.

eight	ate	sea	see
eye	I	hear	here

Write the words in the boxes below.

To learn your new snap words, we'll play a game called **Snap Word Bingo!**

Directions: Have an adult or friend call out snap words from the bingo card below. When you get five snap words in a row, call out "bingo!" Since your bingo card has lots of homophones in it, you can mark both words!

us	here	let	sea	little
eight	look	come	mother	I
eye	from	and	ate	my
get	see	going	yes	got
to	beautiful	but	some	hear

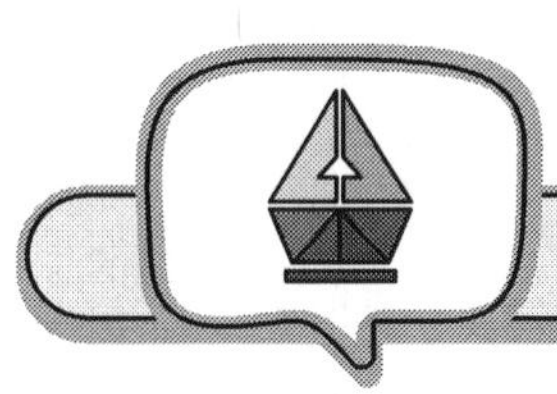

Before you go, review your snap words. If you find one you don't know, **circle** it so you know which words you need to practice!

his	said	saw	say	then
they	but	run	let	us
yes	big	eat	make	take
have	came	same	home	more
not	of	put	your	I'm
into	little	now	three	if
or	read	going	jump	never
there	any	today	very	back
best	just	think	with	than
that				
was	could	from	mother	should
would	don't	away	each	easy
wait	last	near	need	next
been	about	down	house	our
know	school	much	such	two
who	few	because	high	might
over	their	under	want	were
family	find	kind	ask	them
things	walk	eight	ate	sea
see	eye	I	hear	here

WEEK 4

Contractions

We will → we'll

You are → you're

Was not → wasn't

You have → you've

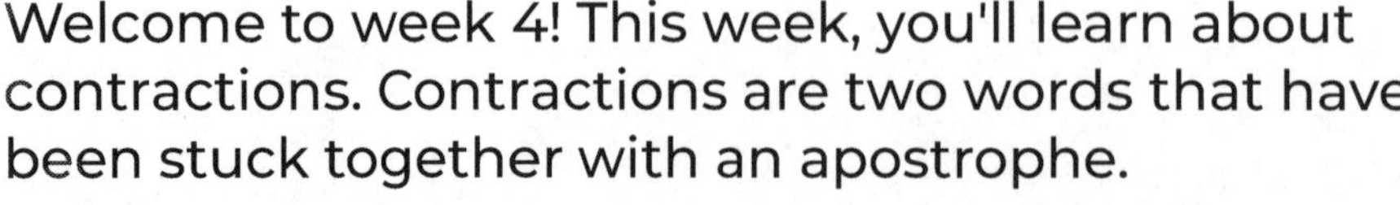

Welcome to week 4! This week, you'll learn about contractions. Contractions are two words that have been stuck together with an apostrophe.

Last week, you learned about **homophones**. Homophones are words that sound the same, but mean two different things!

This week, we'll learn about contractions. **Contractions** are two words that have been stuck together with an apostrophe. An apostrophe looks like this '. It takes the place of the letters that are taken out when the two words are put together.

In fact, two of the homophones you learned about last week are contractions! "You're" is the contraction for "you are," and "they're" is the contraction for "they are."

We use contractions because they are faster to say and write than their expanded forms. With your adult, **read** the list of common contractions below and compare them to their expanded forms.

I am ⟶ I'm	I have ⟶ I've
Do not ⟶ don't	Did not ⟶ didn't
Is not ⟶ isn't	You are ⟶ you're
Can not ⟶ can't	That is ⟶ that's
We will ⟶ we'll	Was not ⟶ wasn't
It is ⟶ it's	You have ⟶ you've

In the activities on the next few pages, you will practice reading and writing contractions.

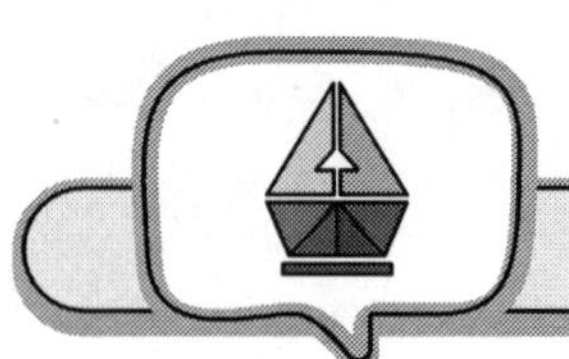

Spin a Contraction

There are a few words that are commonly used in contractions, but not all of them go together!

Directions: Use a pencil and a paper clip to spin and choose a word on both circles. Then, you'll write the two words down and decide if they make a contraction or not. If it makes a contraction, write the contraction the two words make!

An example has been done for you.

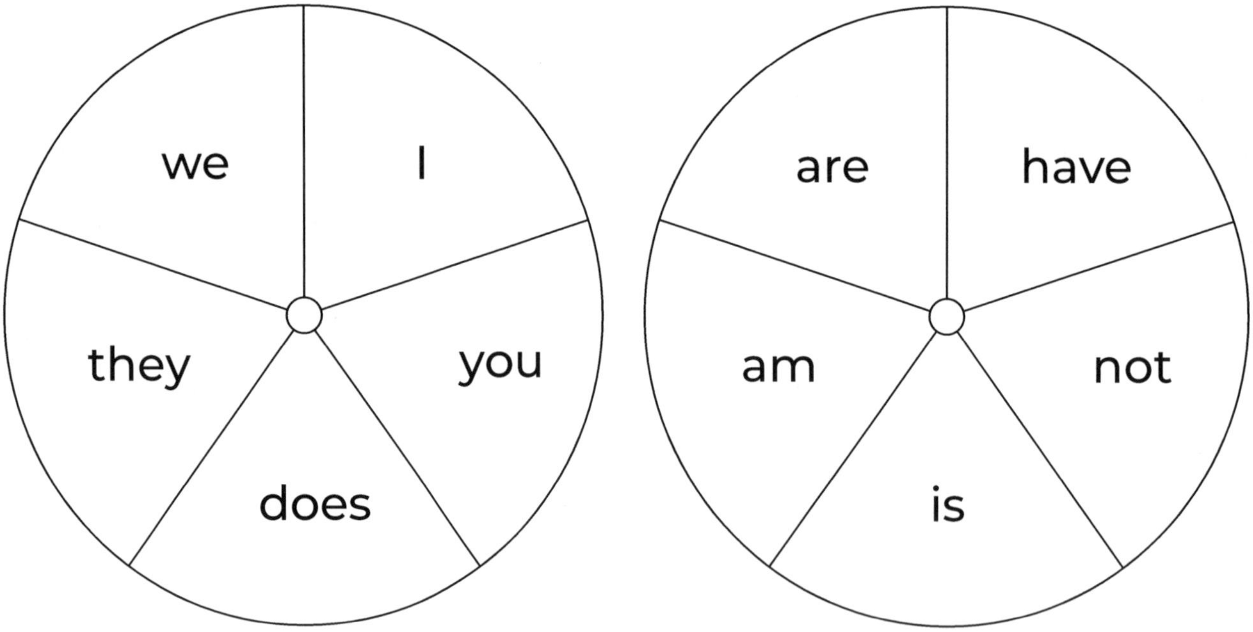

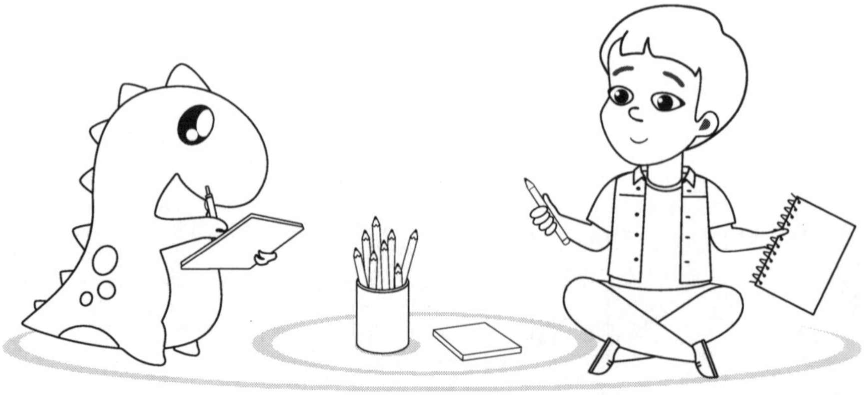

Makes a contraction	Does not make a contraction
we are - we're	does am

Contraction Match

Like you learned in the last activity, not all words make contractions together!

Directions: Color the two words that make a contraction. Then, **write** the contraction on the line. An example has been done for you.

she	not	she
is	here	we
can	are	are

_____she's_____   ________________   ________________

was	they	they
not	can	have
I	are	am

________________   ________________   ________________

Write a sentence with one of the contractions you discovered above!

____

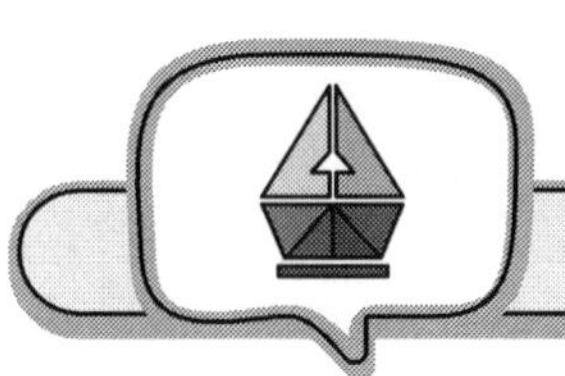

Contraction Maze

Directions: Guide the dog back to his dog house. Start at the top and follow and **shade** in the boxes with two words that make **contractions**.

Do not	they not	You am
You are	We will	Is will
We not	I am	That are
Will not	You have	Could is
You are	They not	I are
They will	Does not	We have

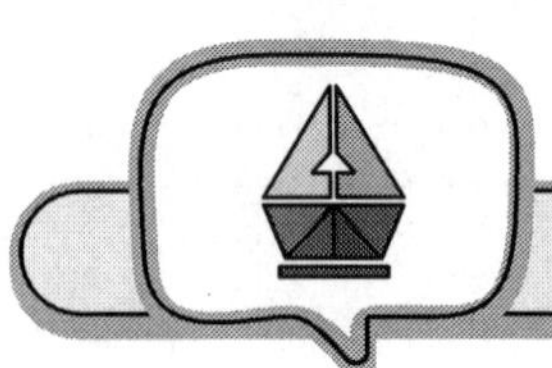

You should have shaded in ten boxes. **Write** the contraction the two words from each box would have made. The first one has been done for you.

1. Don't

2.

3.

4.

5.

6.

7.

8.

9.

10.

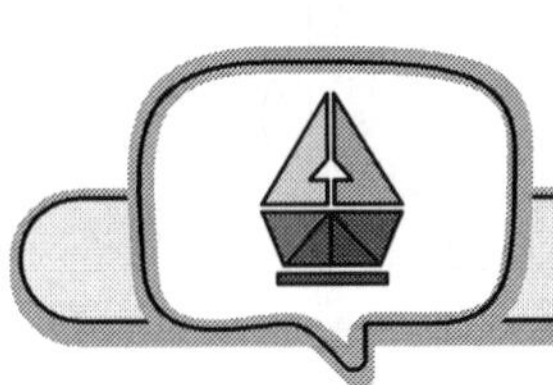

Circle the Contraction Words!

Directions: Read the sentences below. **Circle** the words that can be made into a contraction. Then, rewrite the sentence with the contraction.

1. I can not go to the park.

2. She will not eat peanut butter.

3. He has not brushed his teeth yet.

4. She is going to have fun at the beach!

5. Do you know if they are coming to the party?

6. The dog does not need a new toy.

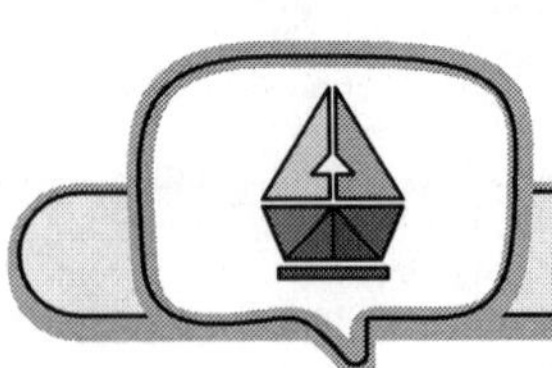

7. They did not see the cat.

8. I am happy the sun is out!

9. We will put on sunscreen.

10. They are very nice.

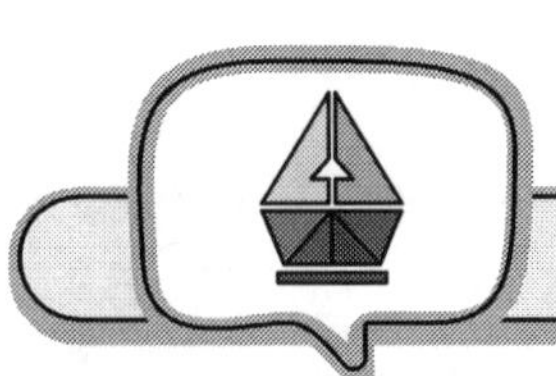

Taking Apart Contractions

Directions: Read the contractions and **write** the two words that make up the contraction. Then, **rewrite** the contraction.

	I've	I have I've
1.	we're	
2.	aren't	
3.	can't	

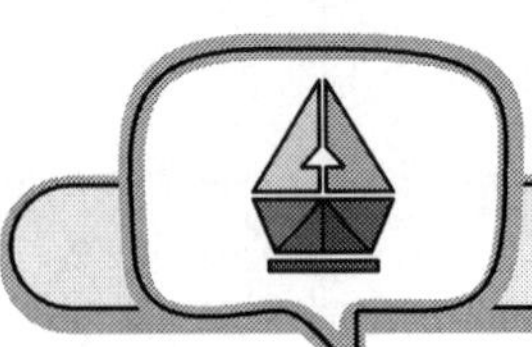

4.	they've	
5.	couldn't	
6.	they're	
7.	they'll	
8.	shouldn't	

9.	I'm	
10.	you're	

We will → we'll
Can not → can't
You are → you're
Was not → wasn't
You have → you've

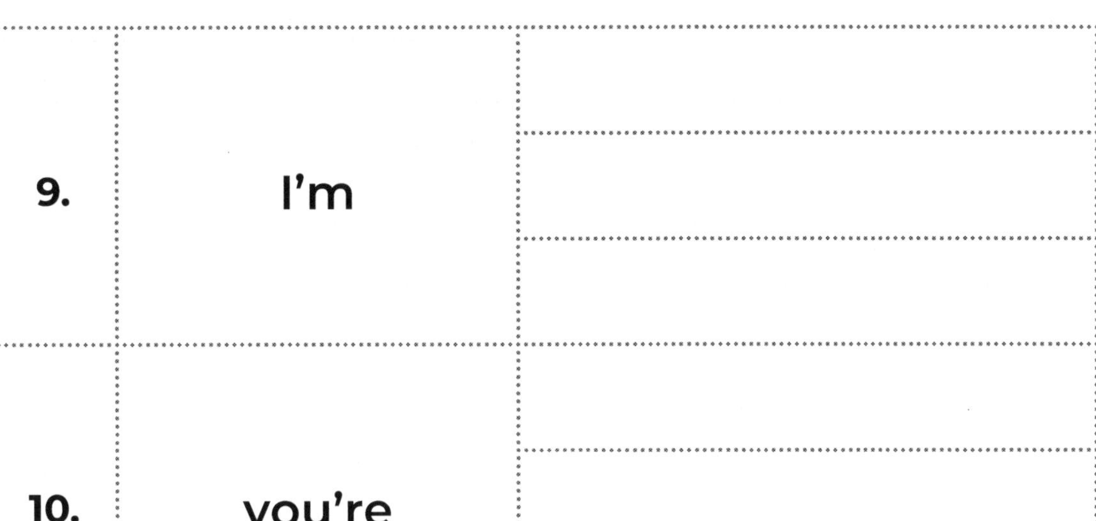

Snap Word Practice

Today we will learn **eight** new snap words! With your adult, read the snap words below.

to	two	too	their
they're	there	you	you're

Did you notice that all of your words for this week are homophones and contractions?

Write the words in the boxes below.

To learn your new snap words, we'll play a game called **Hat Draw Write!**

Directions: Write the numbers 1-8 on pieces of paper. Then, put the pieces of paper into a hat. Draw a number out of the hat, and write the word it corresponds to.

For example, if you draw a 3 out of the hat, write the word "too" in the correct column.

1 - to	2 - two	3 - too	4 - their	5 - they're	6 - there	7 - you	8 - you're

Before you go, review your snap words. If you find one you don't know, **circle** it so you know which words you need to practice!

his	said	saw	say	then
they	but	run	let	us
yes	big	eat	make	take
have	came	same	home	more
not	of	put	your	I'm
into	little	now	three	if
or	read	going	jump	never
there	any	today	very	back

best	just	think	with	than
that				
was	could	from	mother	should
would	don't	away	each	easy
wait	last	near	need	next
been	about	down	house	our
know	school	much	such	two
who	few	because	high	might
over	their	under	want	were
family	find	kind	ask	them
things	walk	eight	ate	sea
see	eye	I	hear	here
to	two	too	you	you're
there	their	they're		

Common, Proper, and Possessive Nouns

This week, you will learn about common, proper, and possessive nouns! This will build on your knowledge of nouns from first grade.

Last week, you learned about **contractions**. Contractions are two words that have been stuck together with an apostrophe.

This week, we'll learn about common, proper, and possessive nouns.

In first grade, you learned that a **noun** is a type of word that names a person, place, or thing. You also learned that a **common noun** is a word that names any person, place, or thing and does not need to be capitalized, while a **proper noun** names a specific person, place, or thing and should always be capitalized.

You'll review **common** and **proper nouns** in this lesson, and you'll learn about **possessive nouns!** Possessive nouns use apostrophes and an s after a noun to show that an object belongs to a noun.

Read the sentence below.

The ball belongs to Billy.

That sentence is sort of long, but making the noun "Billy" possessive can help shorten it up! If we rewrite the sentence with a possessive noun, it would look like this.

The ball is Billy's.

To make the noun "Billy" possessive, we added an apostrophe and an s. You'll get to practice this more later!

In the activities on the next few pages, you will practice identifying, reading, and writing common, proper, and possessive nouns.

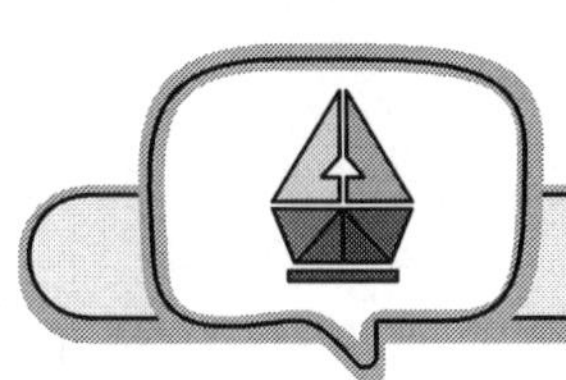

Common and Proper Noun Review

Directions: Read the list of nouns below. Some of the nouns are common nouns and some of the nouns are proper nouns.

day	mountain	corn	turkey	July
cousin	Trisha	girl	Rocky Mountains	United States
doctor	truck	month	Sunday	hotel
president	New York	city	dog	county

Then, **write** the noun in the correct column. An example has been done for you.

Common Noun	Proper Noun
month	July

Common Noun	Proper Noun

Noun Word Search

Directions: Circle the noun in each sentence, and then find it in the word search.

1. The balloon flies high.

2. Frida is nice.

3. The car is on.

4. My blue hat is ripped.

5. The pie is too hot.

6. The carpet is soft.

7. The brown door is open.

8. The dog is dirty.

9. He ate a red apple.

10. The cat is mad.

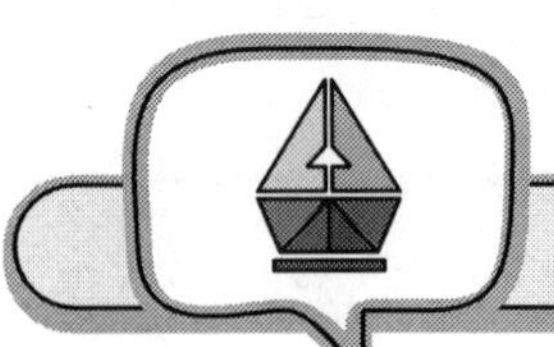

Word Search

C O C P I E C O X O H A
A B A H P D A P P L E D
R J T A B A L L O O N O
P D Q T Q U O I A V F O
E D H Q E D C G W D B R
T H F R I D A C A R Z A
I W T G K M Q D B M D K
F K D O G J X T Y Y B D

Directions: Find the following words in the puzzle.
Words are hidden ➔ and ↓.

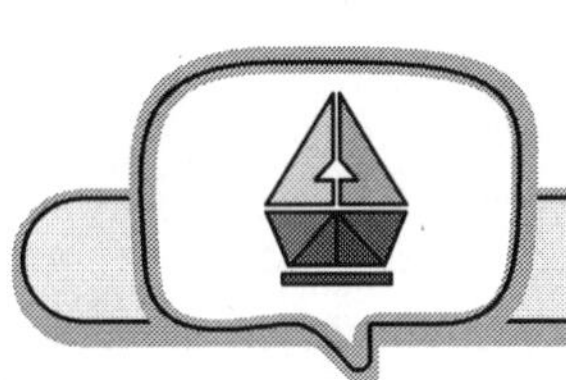

Possessive Nouns

Possessive nouns show something **belongs** to a person, place, or thing. Read the examples of the possessive nouns below.

Shanika's shirt

school's doors

dog's tail

Did you notice that each noun had an apostrophe and an s added to show ownership?

Directions: Read the list of nouns. Then, **write** the possessive noun.

Singular Noun	Possessive Noun
cat	cat's
Mom	
friend	
girl	
boy	
house	
bird	
cow	
Chong	
basement	

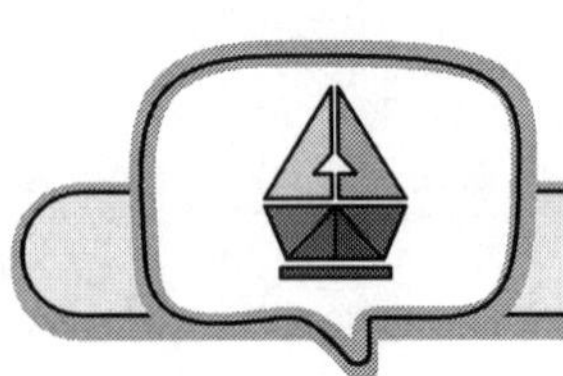 

Replacing the Possessive Noun

Directions: Read the sentences below. **Circle** the correct possessive noun so that the two sentences match. Then, **rewrite** the sentence with the possessive noun.

Example:

That book belongs to my friend. = It's my **friend's** book.

1. That's the house where my grandma lives. = That's my .... house.

   A. grandma's

   B. grandmas

   ....

   ....

2. Our dog always sleeps in that chair. - It's the .... chair.

   A. dogs

   B. dog's

   ....

   ....

3. The party was for her birthday. = The party was for my .... birthday.

   A. moms

   B. mom's

   ....

   ....

4. The trampoline belongs to my sister. = That's my .... trampoline.

   A. sister's

   B. brother's

5. The flowers in the vase have a lovely scent. = The flowers are my ....

   A. sister's

   B. sisters

Using Common, Proper, and Possessive Nouns in Sentences

Common, proper, and possessive nouns have important rules for how they should be written and used in sentences. In this activity, you will write sentences using all three nouns correctly.

Directions: Read the sentences below. **Rewrite** each sentence correctly. If the sentence is already written correctly, circle the nouns in the sentence.

Example:

sharis cat is little.

Shari's cat is little.

1. donald has a pet dog named spot.

2. jerome, Kris, and callie drove to albany.

3. rebeccas scarf got lost on the subway.

4. Vika's bird has its own bedroom.

5. hamilton wants to go to Freddys Burger House for dinner.

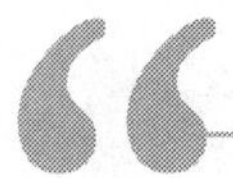

Sentence 4 - was

....

....

Sentence 5 - could

....

....

Before you go, review your snap words. If you find one you don't know, **circle** it so you know which words you need to practice! Your first grade words are **bolded**. This is the last week your first grade words will be on the list, so make sure you know them!

his	said	saw	say	then
they	but	run	let	us
yes	big	eat	make	take
have	came	same	home	more
not	of	put	**your**	I'm
into	little	now	three	if
or	read	going	jump	never
there	any	today	very	back
best	just	think	**with**	than
that				
was	**could**	from	mother	should

would	don't	away	each	easy
wait	last	near	need	next
been	about	down	house	our
know	school	much	such	two
who	few	because	high	might
over	their	under	want	were
family	find	kind	ask	them
things	walk	eight	ate	sea
see	eye	I	hear	here
to	two	too	you	you're
there	their	they're	school	people
cousin	was	could		

WEEK 6

Plural Nouns

This week, you'll continue your noun knowledge by learning about plural nouns! Plural nouns are used when there is more than one of something.

Week 6 — Plural Nouns

Last week, you reviewed **common** and **proper nouns** from first grade, and you learned about **possessive nouns**. Possessive nouns show something belongs to something else.

This week, we'll learn about **plural nouns**. A plural noun is used to show there is more than one of something.

There are a few rules for turning a noun into a plural noun. For most nouns, all you need to do is add an s to the end of the word.

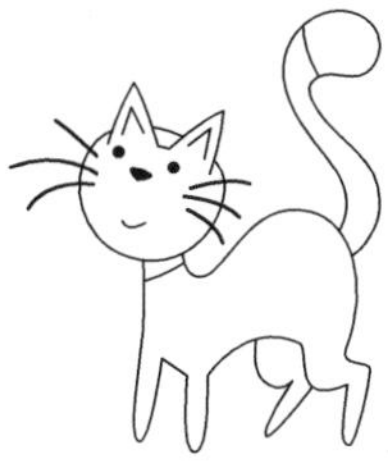	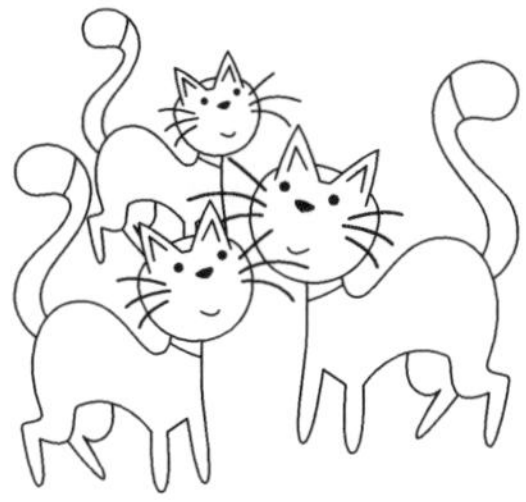	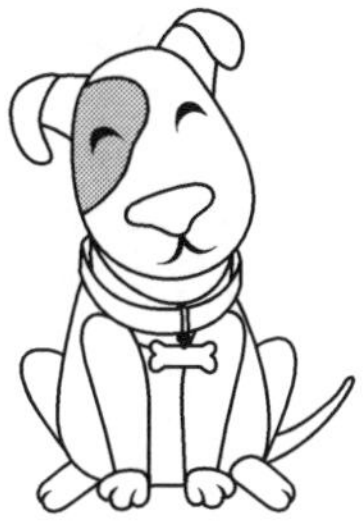	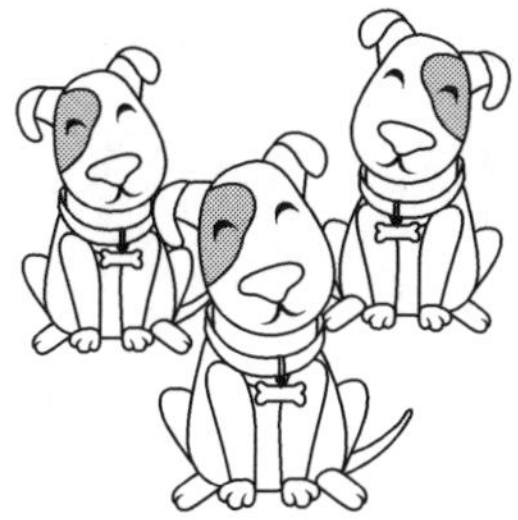
cat	cats	dog	dogs
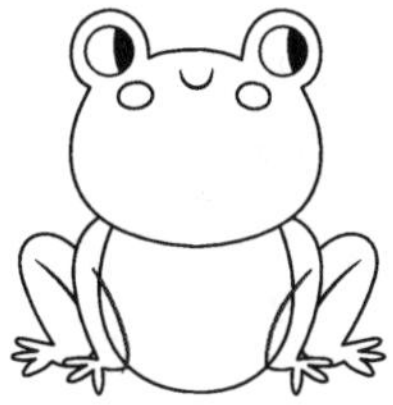	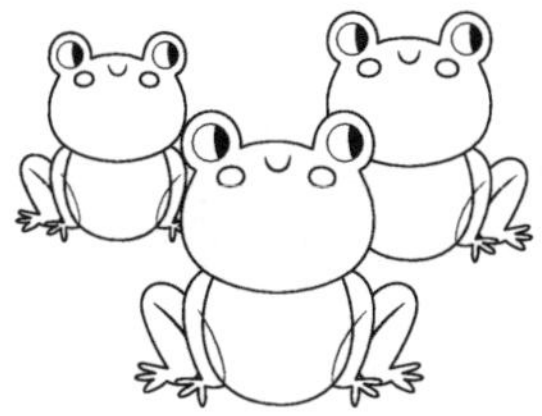		
frog	frogs		

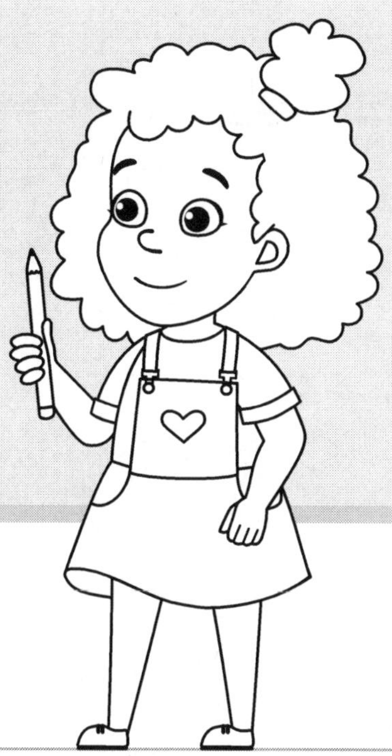

If a noun ends in ch, sh, s, x, or z, you add an es.

If a noun ends in y, you usually add ies.

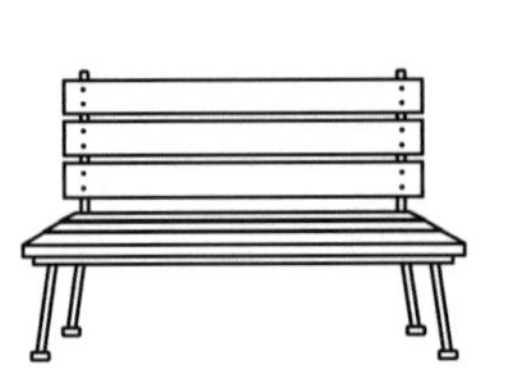

bench

benches

puppy

puppies

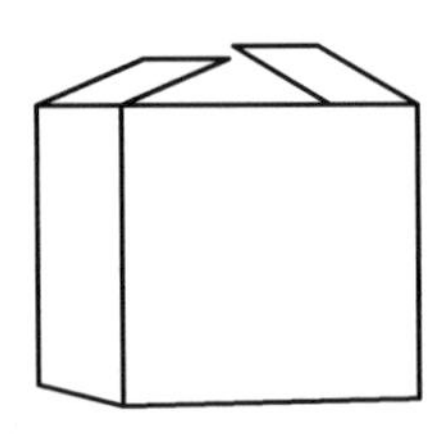

box

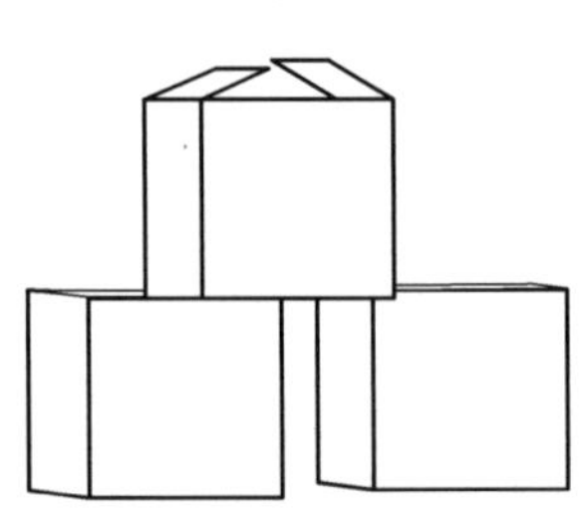

boxes

baby

babies

dish

dishes

penny

pennies

Then, there are some nouns that don't follow rules at all! If there are more than one of these nouns, they change how they are spelled. These are called **irregular plural nouns**.

mouse	mice	child	children
man	men		

In the activities on the next few pages, you will practice identifying, reading, and writing plural nouns.

Regular Plural Nouns

Many plural nouns are regular plural nouns. To create a regular plural noun, add an s onto the end of the word.

Directions: Look at the pictures below. Then, **write** the plural noun they show.

		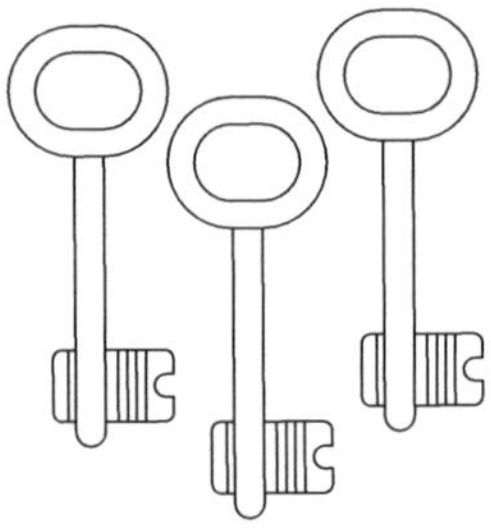	
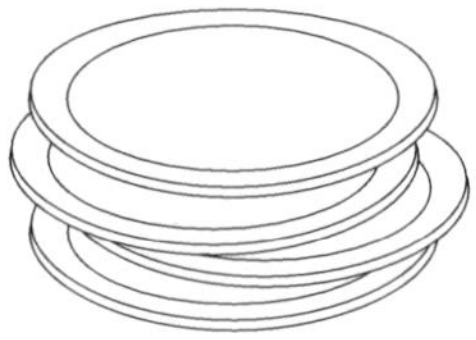		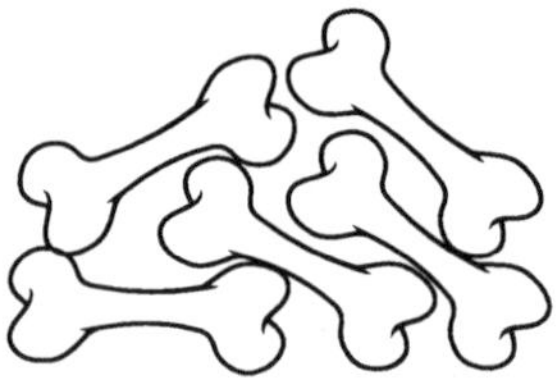	

It is also important to know which noun a plural noun is referring to!
Draw a line to match each noun to its plural noun.

plane	houses
bowl	crayons
rabbit	books
shoe	bowls
house	rabbits
crayon	planes
book	bikes
bike	bananas
banana	desks
desk	shoes

Plural Nouns with -es Maze

If a noun ends in ch, sh, s, x, or z, you add an es.

Directions: Read all of the nouns below. Make them all plural by adding an -s or an -es. Then, guide the dog back to his dog house. Start at the top and follow and shade in the boxes with plural nouns that will end in -es.

The first one has been done for you.

bench**es**	star	book
glass	girl	computer
bus	wish	brush
jet	boy	dress
cord	grape	watch
sock	donkey	couch

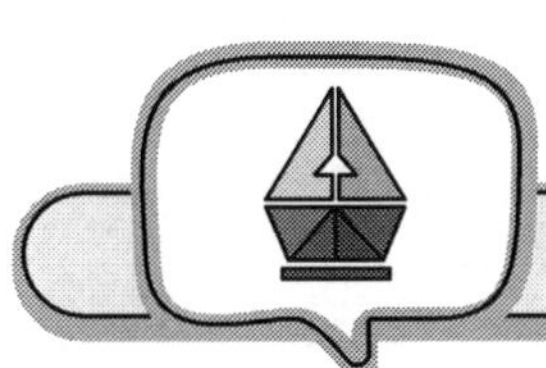 

You should have shaded in eight boxes. **Write** the plural nouns you followed to get the dog home. The first one has been done for you.

1. benches

2.

3.

4.

5.

6.

7.

8.

Plural Nouns with -ies

Do you remember at the beginning of this week when we said nouns that end in y usually have -ies added to make them plural? That's because the letter that comes before the y has to be a consonant to make this rule work.

For instance, the plural of the word "monkey" is "monkeys" because the letter that comes before the y is a vowel.

To make a noun that follows this rule plural, you have to replace the y with -ies. This is a little different than our other nouns, because we're taking away a letter! For example, "puppy" becomes "puppies."

Directions: Read the list of words below. Rewrite the word and add the correct ending to make it plural.

The first one has been done for you.

monkey	monkeys
butterfly	
pony	
donkey	
supply	
holiday	
fairy	
boy	
raspberry	
story	
family	

There are some nouns that don't follow the rules at all when they are plural! It can be hard to memorize them all, so here are the ones you will probably see most when you are reading and writing.

Singular Noun	Plural Noun
child	children
man	men
woman	women
foot	feet
goose	geese
person	people
mouse	mice

Use each of the irregular plural nouns to write a sentence.

1. ____

2. ____

3. ____

4. ____

5. ____

6. ____

7. ____

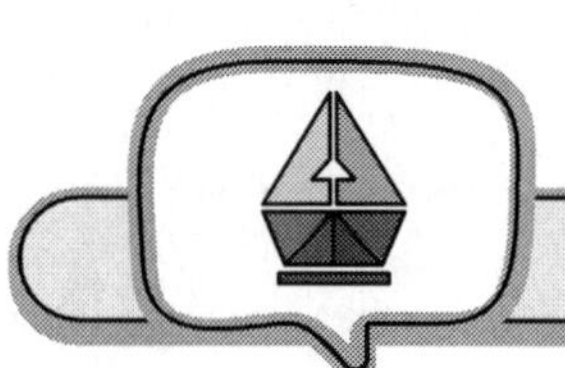

Correcting Plural Noun Sentences

Directions: Read the sentences below. **Rewrite** each sentence correctly. Pay attention to how the nouns are pluralized!

1. Mouses like cheese.

2. The childs play on the playground.

3. Her shoeses are too small for her foots.

4. My parents gave me two new toyies for my birthday.

5. I want some strawberres and peachies with my lunch.

Week 6 • Activity 6

Snap Word Practice

Today we will learn **five** new snap words! With your adult, read the snap words below.

better   **follow**   **happen**   **different**   **very**

Write the words in the boxes below.

To learn your new snap words, we'll play a game called **Snap Word Scramble!**

Directions: Look at the list of scrambled letters in each box. Unscramble the letters and **write** the snap word they make.

epnpah	yrve	ttrbee	lfowol	ttrbee
reeftdfni	lloowf	yrev	defnrietf	epnpah

This week, you will learn about a new type of word: compound words! Compound words may look long and scary, but by the end of this week, you'll be a compound word pro!

Last week, you learned about **plural nouns**. A plural noun is used to show there is more than one of something, but there are a few rules to follow when you're writing them.

This week, we'll learn about **compound words**. A compound word is two words stuck together! They can trip you up when you're reading because they look long and scary, but once you learn to see the two words inside a compound word, they're a piece of cake!

When you see a compound word, it has a new meaning!

Butter + fly = Butterfly

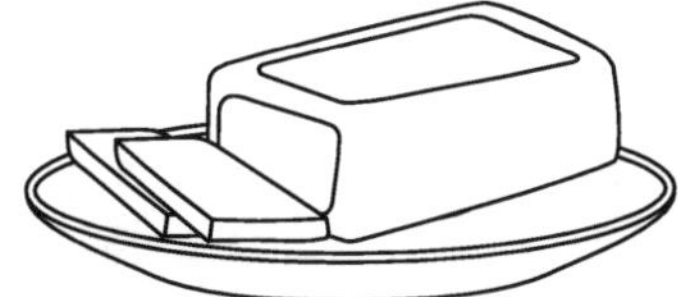

In the activities on the next few pages, you will practice reading and writing compound words.

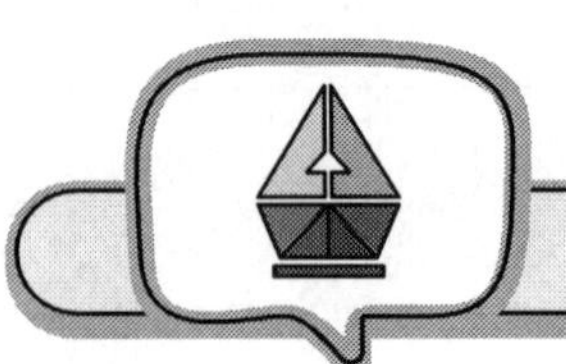 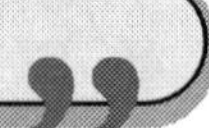

Reading Compound Words

Directions: Read the compound words. **Circle** the two words you see inside the compound word. Then, **draw** a picture to match each word.

butterfly	strawberry	cowgirl	snowman
cupcake	baseball	blackbird	birdhouse
popcorn		rainbow	

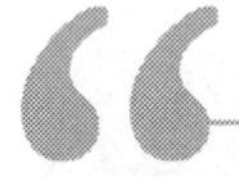

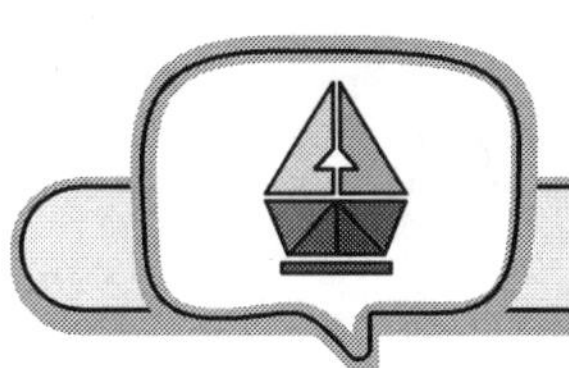

Writing Compound Words

Directions: Look at the pictures below. Write the compound word they show. An example has been completed for you.

(sword)	+ (fish)	=	swordfish
(sun)	+ (glasses)	=	
(rain)	+ (coat)	=	
(gold)	+ (fish)	=	
(snow)	+ (man)	=	
(dragon)	+ (fly)	=	

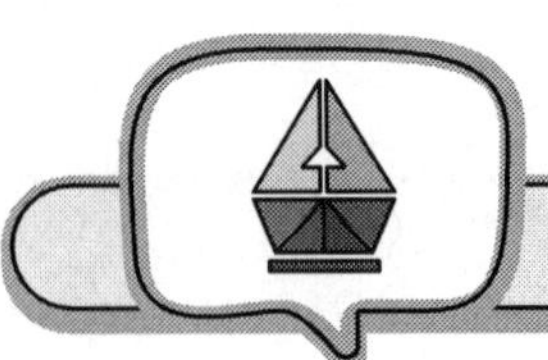

Compound Word Work

homework

Directions: Complete each compound word chart like the example below.

Word 1: home	Word 2: work
	Compound Word: homework	
Sentence: Shania did her homework after dinner.	

Word 1:		Word 2:
	Compound Word:	
Sentence: Greta turned on her flashlight in the dark room.		Picture

Word 1:		Word 2:
	Compound Word: eyeball	
Sentence:		Picture

Word 1:		Word 2:
	Compound Word:	
Sentence: The teapot whistled on the stove.		Picture

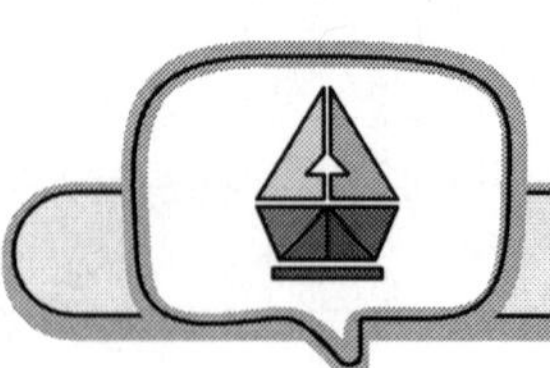

Word 1: egg		Word 2: shell
	Compound Word: eggshell	
Sentence:		Picture

Word 1:		Word 2:
	Compound Word: snowball	
Sentence:		Picture

Word Search

Directions: Complete the word search. Circle the smaller words you see inside the compound words.

```
A N E W S P A P E R F W
M O O N L I G H T S N E
T C L A S S R O O M Z E
B B R E A K F A S T H K
U G N B A S E B A L L E
H B U T T E R F L Y X N
O T O O T H B R U S H D
J U A I R P L A N E B N
```

Directions: Find the following words in the puzzle.

Words are hidden ➡ and ⬇.

AIRPLANE	BUTTERFLY	NEWSPAPER
BASEBALL	CLASSROOM	TOOTHBRUSH
BREAKFAST	MOONLIGHT	WEEKEND

Snap Word Practice

Today we will learn **four** new snap words! With your adult, read the snap words below.

somewhere   **anyone**   **nobody**   **outside**

Did you notice that all of your snap words this week are compound words?

Write the words in the boxes below.

To learn your new snap words, we'll play a game called **Snap Word Bingo!**

Directions: Have an adult or friend call out snap words from the bingo card below. When you get five snap words in a row, call out "bingo!" Since your bingo card has lots of homophones in it, you can mark both words!

little	know	outside	us	here
people	family	come	eight	look
anyone	because	and	they're	nobody
got	somewhere	going	get	see
hear	school	but	to	beautiful

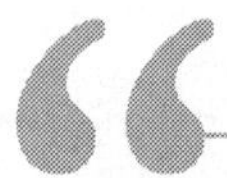

Root Words, Prefixes, and Suffixes

This week you'll use what you learned in first grade about root words! You'll learn about adding prefixes to words to change their meaning.

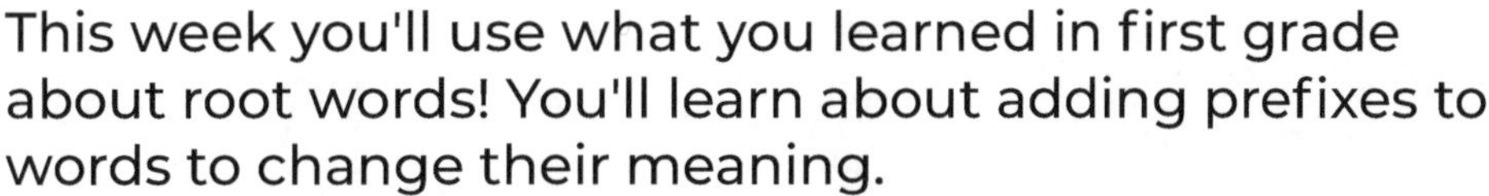

Root Words, Prefixes, and Suffixes

In first grade, you learned about **root words** and **suffixes**. A **root word** is a word that has a meaning all by itself. Jump, play, and run are all root words. A **suffix** is a part of a word that gets added on to the end of a root word that changes what it means.

In second grade, you are going to learn how to add **prefixes** onto your root words! A **prefix** is a part of a word that gets added onto the beginning of a root word that changes what it means.

You'll learn a few prefixes in this lesson, but let's look at a quick example!

The prefix "mis" means wrong. So what happens if we add it to the word "spell?"

mis + spell = misspell

Now, the word means "spelled wrong!"

Read the chart below with your adult.

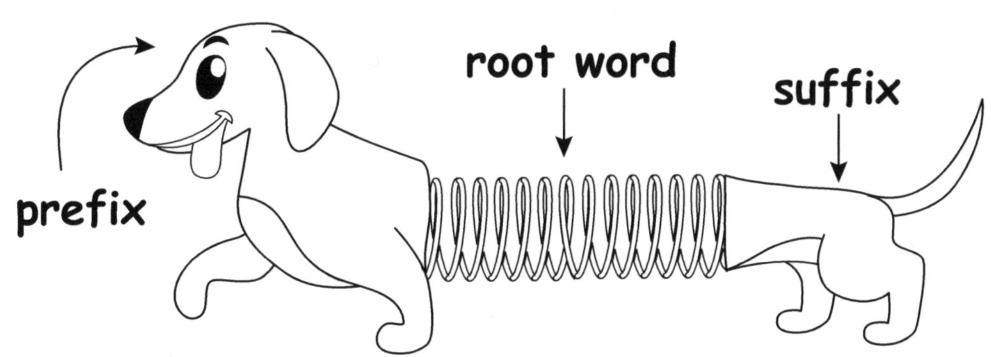

Prefix → **Root word** ← **Suffix**

A word added to the **beginning** of a root word

A word added to the **end** of a root word

Prefix = Meaning
re = again
un = not
pre = before
dis = not

Suffix = Meaning
ful = ful of
ly = like
less = without
ness = being
est = most
er = someone who or more

In the activities on the next few pages, you will practice reading and writing prefixes and suffixes words.

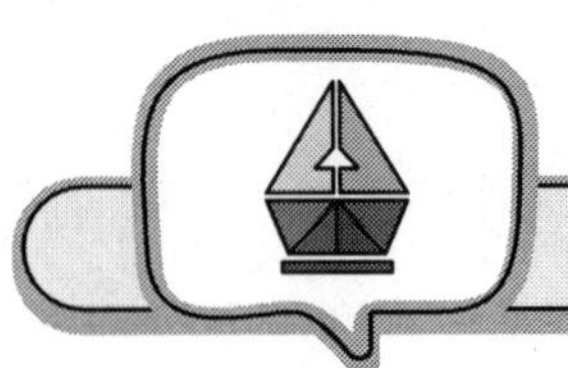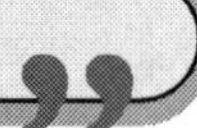

Prefixes

Prefixes come before root words. There are lots of prefixes, but we'll be learning about the prefixes un-, pre-, dis-, and re- in second grade.

Read the prefixes and their meanings below.

un-	pre-	dis-	re-
not	before	not	again

Directions: : **Read** the words below. **Underline** the prefix. Then, **write** what the word means. The first two have been done for you.

<u>un</u>happy	not happy
<u>pre</u>heat	heat before
dislike	
rename	
unlock	
reread	
disobey	
unable	
preview	
rearrange	
distrust	
preown	

Week 8 • Activity 2

Suffixes

You learned a few suffixes in first grade. A **suffix** is a part of a word that gets added on to the end of a root word that changes what it means.

Read the suffixes and their meanings below.

-ful	-ly	-less	-ness	-est	-er
full of	like	without	being	most	someone who/more

Directions: : **Read** the words below. **Underline** the suffix. Then, **write** what the word means. The first two have been done for you.

wonder<u>ful</u>	full of wonder
teach<u>er</u>	A person who teaches
coldest	
stronger	
powerful	
happiness	
playful	
helper	
fearless	
player	
quickest	
helpless	

Root Words

Root words are the first kind of word you learned to read and write! Prefixes and suffixes may change what root words mean, but they aren't actually words all by themselves. It is important to be able to pull the root word out of any word.

Directions: Read the list of words below. **Underline** the root word in each word. Then, rewrite the sentence without using prefixes or suffixes.

Example:

Mom pre<u>paid</u> for the food on the app.

Mom paid for the food on the app before we picked it up.

1. The cat disappeared!

____

2. My grandma is the nicest lady in the world.

____

3. I am quicker than my brother.

____

4. The video was unable to load.

____

5. My grandpa is fearless!

____

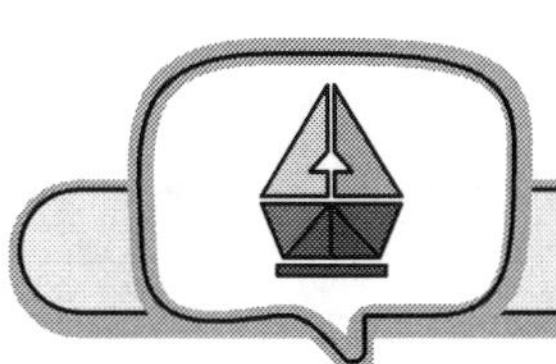

Make Your Own Words!

Directions: Use the list prefixes, root words, and suffixes to make your own words! Be sure to write what they mean. The words can be real words or made up words.

un-	pre-	dis-	re-
not	before	not	again

Root Words

play	jump
walk	read
sleep	build
eat	wash
draw	think

-ful	-ly	-less	-ness	-est	-er
full of	like	without	being	most	someone who/more

The first one has been completed for you.

prefix/suffix	Word	meaning
-less	sleepless	Without sleep

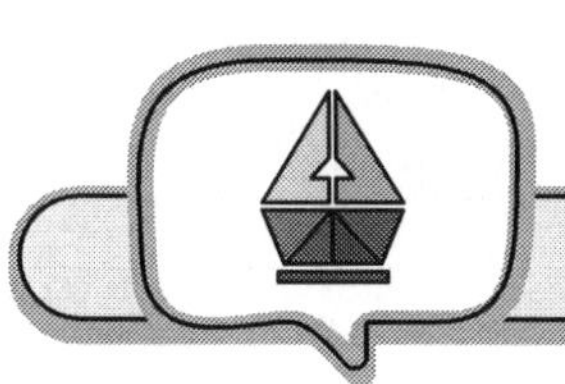

Prefix and Suffix Quiz

1. A prefix comes .... a root word.

   A. after

   B. before

2. A suffix comes .... a root word

   A. after

   B. before

3. Prefixes and suffixes are words by themselves.

   A. true

   B. false

4. Which prefix means "again?"

   A. pre-

   B. re-

   C. dis-

   D. un-

5. What does the word "suddenly" mean based on its suffix?

   A. To do something in a slow manner.

   B. To do something with great skill.

   C. To do something in a quick and unexpected way.

   D. To do something that is seen or heard.

Snap Word Practice

Today we will learn **five** new snap words! With your adult, read the snap words below.

| question | slowly | suddenly |
| probably | usually | |

Write the words in the boxes below.

To learn your new snap words, we'll play a game called **Rainbow Write!**

Directions: Get some crayons or markers and write each of your words in rainbow colors.

question	slowly	suddenly	probably	usually

WEEK 9

Verb Agreement: Make it Make Sense!

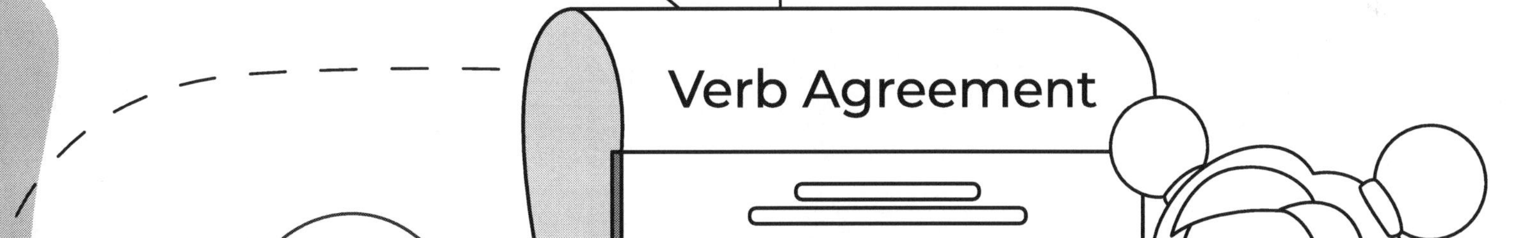

Verb Agreement

1
2
3

This week you'll learn about verb agreement! When verbs and nouns agree in a sentence, the sentence makes sense.

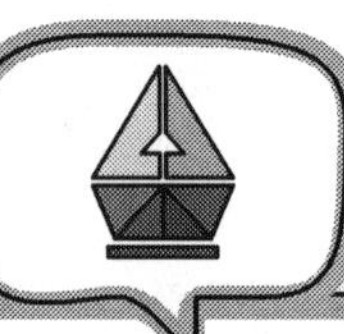

Last week, you learned about **prefixes**, **suffixes**, and **root words**. **Prefixes** and **suffixes** are word parts that go onto **root words** to change their meaning.

This week, you'll be learning about **verb agreement**. Verb agreement sounds like a fancy term, but you probably already know what it means! **Verb agreement** means that all of the words in a sentence need to work together to make it make sense!

First, let's review what a verb is. A **verb** is a type of word. Verbs describe what a noun is doing.

Read the sentences below. The verbs are underlined.

The boy <u>runs</u> across the playground.

I am <u>swimming</u> in the pool.

The dog <u>jumps</u> over the fence.

All of the sentences above made sense. But what if the first sentence said, "The boy <u>run</u> across the playground."? That wouldn't make any sense! The **verb** doesn't agree with the noun, so the sentence sounds strange.

Thankfully, there are some rules for verb agreement, so we don't have to guess.

If the noun in the sentence is singular, add an -s to the **verb**.

* A <u>rabbit</u> eat**s** grass.

If the <u>noun</u> is plural OR if the noun is I or you, **don't** add an -s to the **verb**!

* The <u>rabbits</u> **eat** grass.

* <u>You</u> don't **eat** grass.

In the activities on the next few pages, you will practice more with **verb agreement**.

Which Verb?

Directions: Read the sentences below. **Circle** the verb that correctly fills in the blank. Then, **write** the verb on the line. The first one has been completed for you.

1. My mom *bakes* cakes.

   A. bakes

   B. bake

   bakes

2. Mark .... to the party.

   A. go

   B. goes

3. The dog .... wet.

   A. am

   B. is

4. Our friends .... a lot of pizza.

   A. eats

   B. eat

5. The girls .... on the swings.

   A. play

   B. plays

6. The apples .... in the bag.

    A. is   **B.** are

....

7. Mrs. Jahng .... funny stories.

    A. tells   **B.** tell

....

8. She .... on the trampoline.

    A. jump   **B.** jumps

....

9. Gregorio .... my best friend.

    A. am   **B.** is

....

10. I can .... my book tonight.

    A. read   **B.** reads

....

Week 9 • Activity 2

Spin the Verb

Nouns and verbs must agree in a sentence, otherwise, they don't make sense!

Directions: Use a pencil and a paper clip to spin and choose a word on both circles. Then, you'll write the two words down and decide if they agree or not.

An example has been done for you.

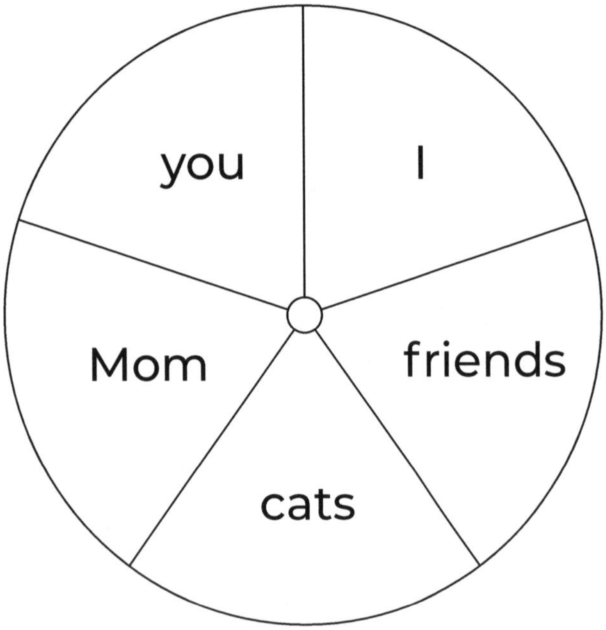

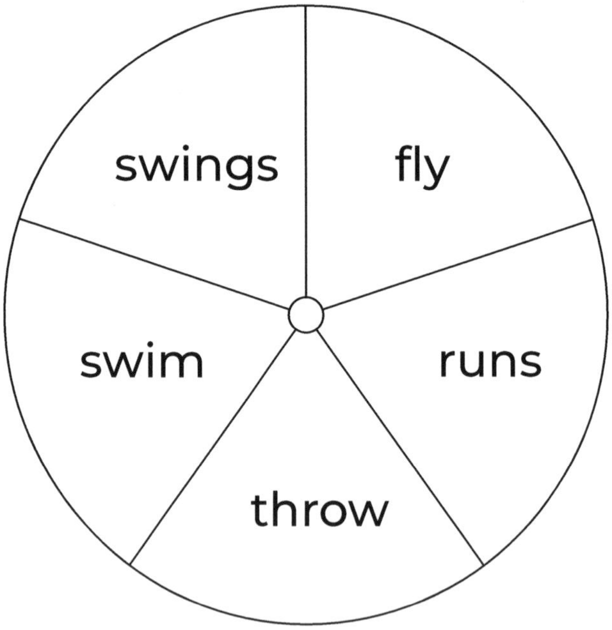

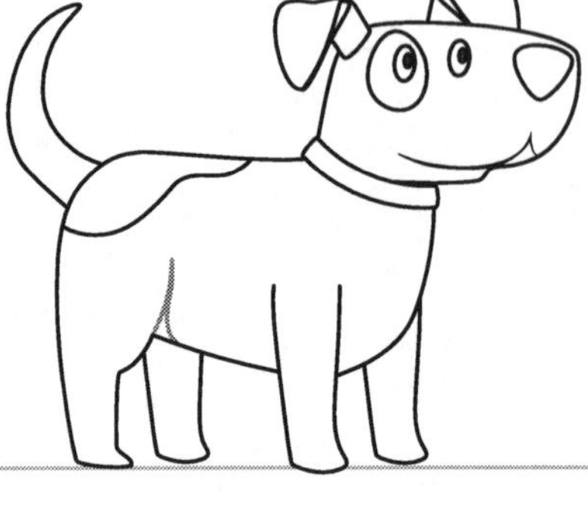

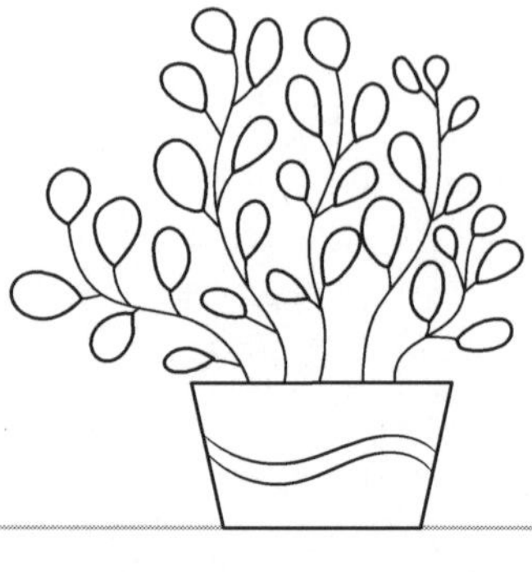

Agrees	Does not agree
I swim	Cats runs

Verb Agreement Maze

Directions: Guide the dog back to his dog house. Start at the top and follow and shade in the boxes with the correct verb agreement.

she is	We swims	I cries
they swim	Greg think	He climb
Mom reads	I eat	James paint
You plays	We run	I drives
Grandpa cook	Trevor and Mary listen	Ms. Creasy teaches
Frida dance	My aunt talk	I laugh

You should have shaded in eight boxes. **Write** a sentence with one of the verb agreements you colored in above.

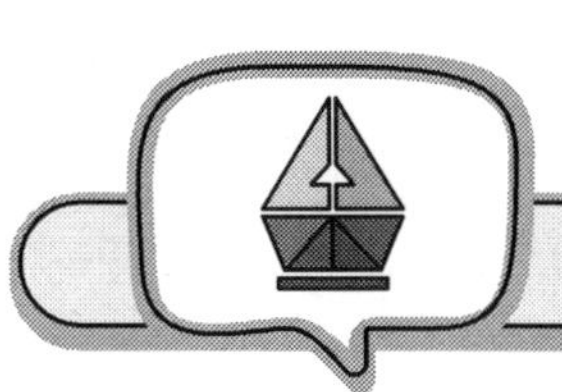

Verb Agreement Sentences

Directions: Read the sentences below. **Rewrite** each sentence correctly.

1. My mom walk the dog.

2. Callie see the fresh pie.

3. Did you goes to the game?

4. Can Marco and Kiara plays tag?

5. I loves to eat pizza!

6. We paints the wall.

7. You dances very well.

8. My uncle drive us to school.

9. My sisters sleeps in the same room.

10. I reads every night.

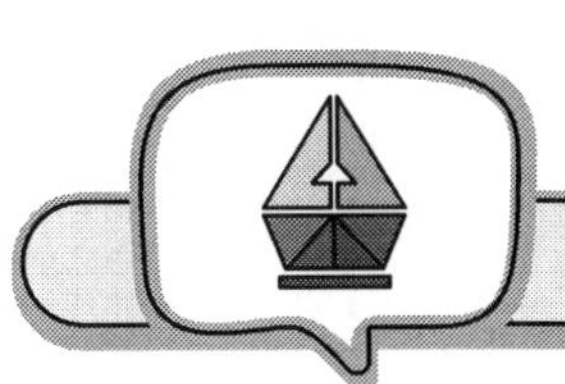

Match a Noun

So far, you've been making sure the verb matches the noun in the sentence, but now, you'll be able to pick your own noun! It is up to you if you'd like for the sentences to be silly or serious.

Directions: Fill in each blank with a noun that matches the verb in the sentence. The first one has been done for you.

1. The <u>dog</u> barks loudly when the mail carrier arrives.

2. The .... sing songs in the school choir.

3. The .... sleeps on the windowsill.

4. The .... study for their test.

5. The .... chirp in the morning.

6. The .... speeds down the highway.

7. The .... bloom in the garden.

8. The .... teaches the lesson.

9. The .... belong to the library.

10. The .... works well.

Snap Word Practice

Today we will learn **five** new snap words! With your adult, read the snap words below.

answer	goes	does
begin	trouble	

Write the words in the boxes below.

To learn your new snap words, we'll play a game called **Highlighter Write!**

Directions: Use a pencil or a pen to write your new words. Then, trace over each word with a highlighter.

Example: monkey, melon

Your turn! Use all your words and play the **Highlighter Snap Word** game.

Before you go, review your snap words. If you find one you don't know, **circle** it so you know which words you need to practice!

eight	ate	see	sea	here
hear	I	eye	hear	here
to	two	too	you	you're
there	their	they're	school	people
cousin	was	could	better	follow
happen	different	very	somewhere	anyone
nobody	outside	question	slowly	suddenly
probably	usually	answer	goes	does
begin	trouble			

Adjectives and Adverbs

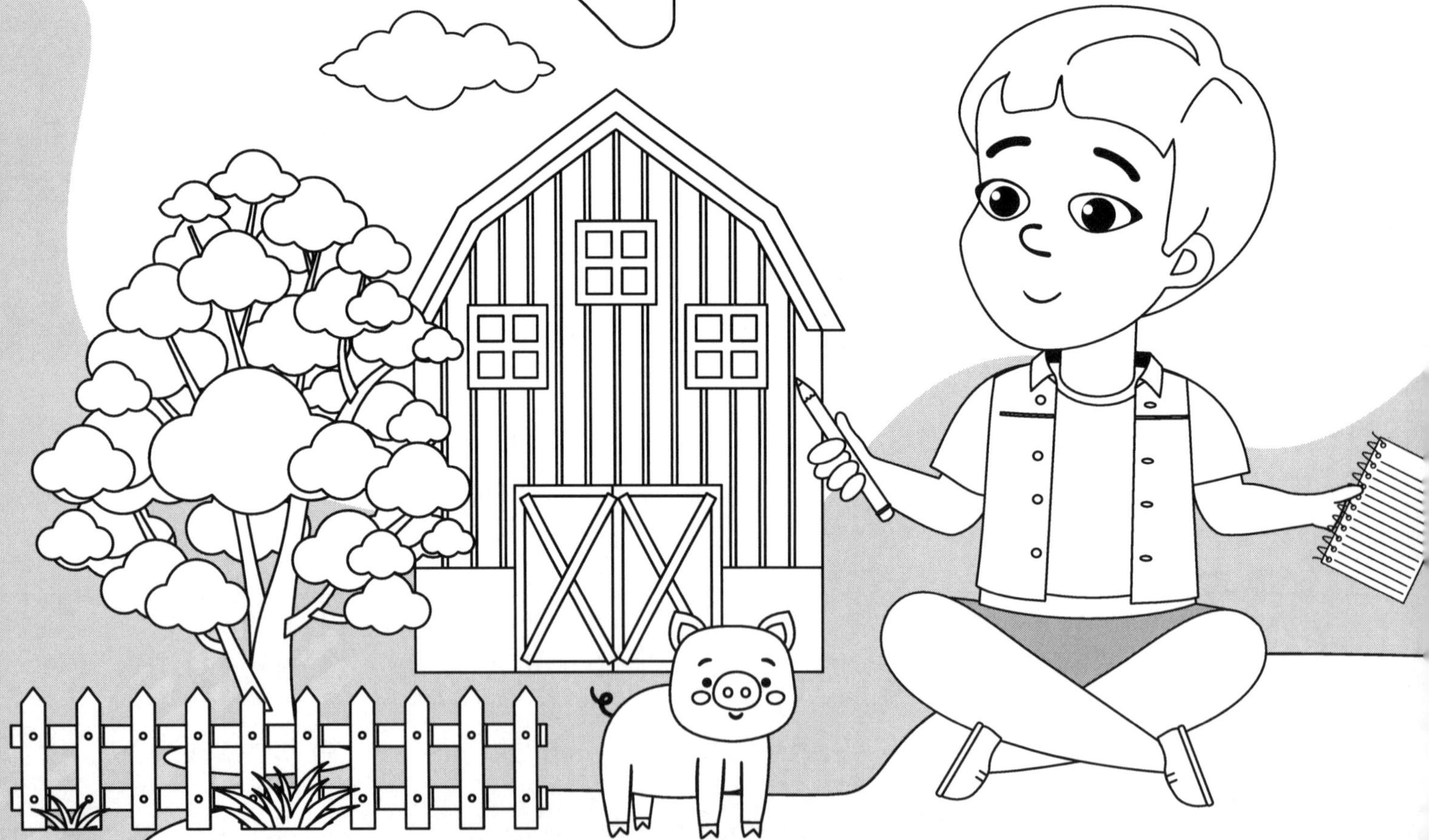

This week, you'll learn about more special kinds of words: adjectives and adverbs! When you finish this week, you'll be able to use adjectives and adverbs to make your writing more interesting.

Last week, you learned about **verb agreement, which means** that all of the words in a sentence need to work together to make it make sense!

This week, you'll be learning about adjectives and **adverbs**. Adjectives and adverbs are both types of describing words. **Adjectives** describe nouns, and **adverbs** describe verbs.

Read the chart below.

What Does it Tell Us?		
Adjectives		**Adverbs**
The color		How
The size		When
How many		Where
What it looks like		How often
What it sounds like		
How it acts		
How it feels		

In the activities on the next few pages, you will learn more about adjectives and adverbs.

Adjective or Not?

Adjectives tell us about nouns. Remember, a **noun** is a person, place, or thing. Adjectives can help make sentences more interesting and help a reader understand more about the noun!

Read the two sentences below and see what you notice.

1. I see the lion.

2. I see the big, hungry lion.

The adjectives "big" and "hungry" make a difference! In the activity below, you'll decide which words are adjectives and which words are not.

It can be hard to tell which words are adjectives, but here's a trick! See if the word makes sense to describe yourself. "I am a nice friend," makes sense, but "I am a dog friend," does not.

Directions: Read the list of words below. **Circle** the words that are adjectives. Then, **write** some sentences with a few of the adjectives.

bright	wet	fast	tree
friend	pen	rug	bumpy
bug	tall	sock	cat
kind	desk	ball	loud

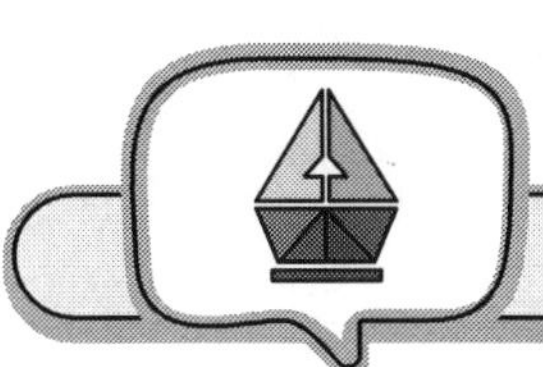

1. ____

2. ____

3. ____

4. ____

5. ____

6. ____

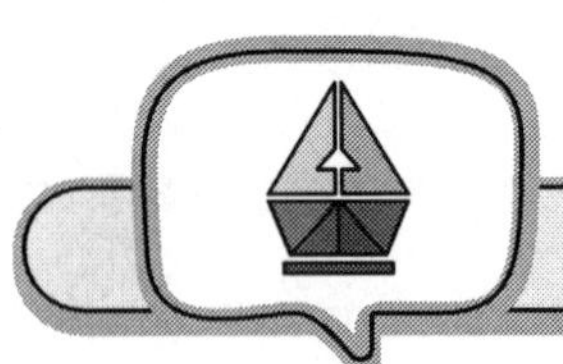

Adjective Sort

Adjectives can be used for all sorts of things, and they make writing and reading more interesting! But not all adjectives go with all words.

Directions: Use the words in the word bank and **write** them next to the correct picture. An example has been done for you.

Word Bank: soft, loud, scary, yummy, cold, strong, sweet, striped, funny, little, friendly, fluffy

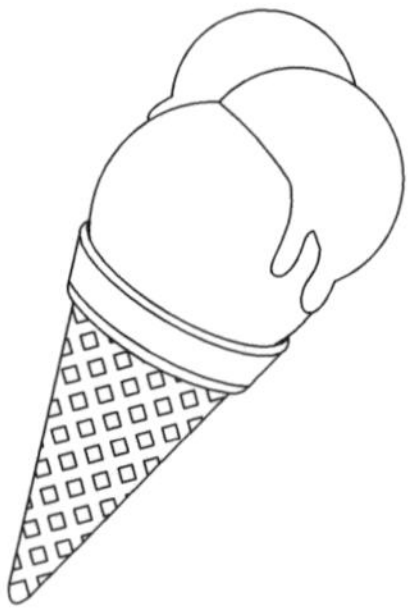	cold

Now, **write** a sentence about one of the pictures above using a new adjective! Draw a picture to match your sentence.

Adverbs

As you reviewed in the last activity, a **verb** is something a noun does. **Adverbs** describe how, when, or where the noun does a verb!

To find adverbs, it is important that you can find the noun and the verb in a sentence.

Directions: Underline the noun and the verb. Then, **circle** the adverb and **write** it on your own. An example has been done for you.

We played today.	today
The bird flew away.	
I cry sometimes.	
You eat slowly.	
I went down the slide.	
My mom carefully fixed the car.	
The princess gracefully walked.	
The snowman melted fast.	

My dad quietly laid my sister down for a nap.	
Sharks swim fast.	
Drake hit the ball easily.	

Add Detail with Adverbs

Adverbs can give us more detail about what is happening in a story.

Directions: Add adverbs to the boxes below to give more detail about what happened. Underline the adverb you add. An example has been done for you.

The cow mooed.
How: The cow mooed **quietly.**
When: The cow mooed **in the morning**.
Where: The cow mooed **in the barn**.
How often: The cow moos **all the time**.

The chicken clucked.
How:
When:
Where:
How often:

The dog barked.

How:

When:

Where:

How often:

The duck quacked.

How:

When:

Where:

How often:

Write an Interesting Sentence

You've learned that every sentence has to have a noun and a verb to make sense, but now you've learned that adjectives and adverbs can make sentences more exciting!

Directions: Rewrite each sentence with an adjective, adverb, or both! An example has been done for you.

1. I see a cat.

   I see a gray cat walk slowly.

2. She wants an ice cream.

3. Hugo threw the ball.

4. The balloon floats.

5. An otter swims.

6. Rita wears a dress.

7. We have spaghetti.

8. I hug my teddy bear.

9. They eat cake.

10. A pig oinks.

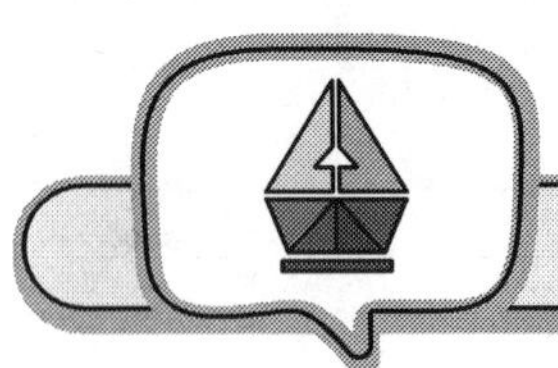 

Snap Word Practice

Today we will learn **five** new snap words! With your adult, read the snap words below.

special	great	excited

beautiful	old

Did you notice that all of your words this week were adjectives?

Write the words in the boxes below.

To learn your new snap words, we'll play a game called **Snap Word Sentences**!

Directions: Use your snap words to **write** sentences. Write one sentence using each snap word.

Example: here

My mom is here.

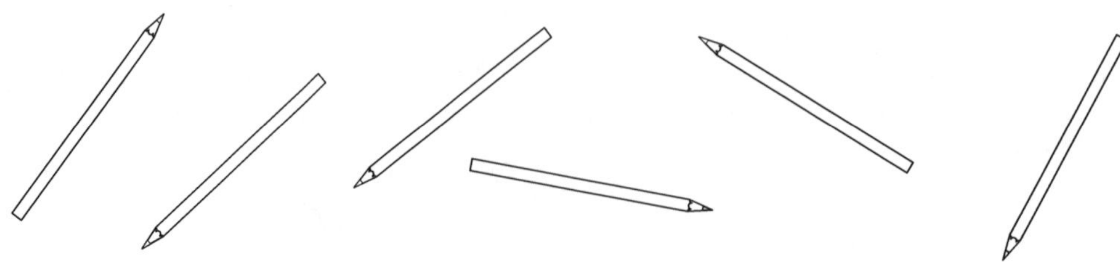

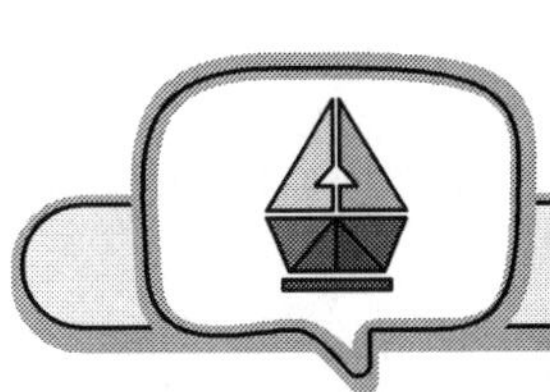

1. ____

2. ____

3. ____

4. ____

5. ____

Before you go, review your snap words. If you find one you don't know, **circle** it so you know which words you need to practice!

eight	ate	see	sea	here
hear	I	eye	hear	here
to	two	too	you	you're
there	their	they're	school	people
cousin	was	could	better	follow
happen	different	very	somewhere	anyone
nobody	outside	question	slowly	suddenly
probably	usually	answer	goes	does
begin	trouble	special	great	excited
beautiful	old			

WEEK 11

Half Time Review

This week you will take a quick break from learning new things. You'll spend some time reviewing all of the things you've learned so far.

You have learned so many amazing things about being a second grade reader and writer, but before you learn more, let's review what you've learned so far.

You started out by reviewing some important first grade reading concepts like **blends, digraphs, vowel teams, and r-controlled vowels.**

Then, you used all your knowledge about reading to learn more about how to be a great writer and speller. Here's a quick summary of what you learned.

* A **homophone** is a word that sounds the same as another word, but it means something different. (Week 3)

* **Contractions** are two words that have been stuck together with an apostrophe. (Week 4)

* You reviewed **common** and **proper nouns**, and you learned that a **possessive noun** uses and apostrophe and an s after a noun to show that an object belongs to a noun. (Week 5)

* A **plural noun** is used to show that there is more than one of something, and you learned some special rules for making nouns plural. (Week 6)

* **Compound words** are two words stuck together. (Week 7)

* A **root word** is a word that has a meaning all by itself. **Prefixes** and **suffixes** are word parts that can be added onto a root word to change what it means. (Week 8)

* **Verb agreement** means that all of the words in a sentence need to work together to make it make sense. (Week 9)

* **Adjectives** describe nouns, and **adverbs** describe verbs. (Week 10)

That's a lot to learn in such a short time!

In the activities on the next few pages, you will get to practice more with each concept. If you need any help, you can always go back to the week the concept was introduced and get a quick refresher.

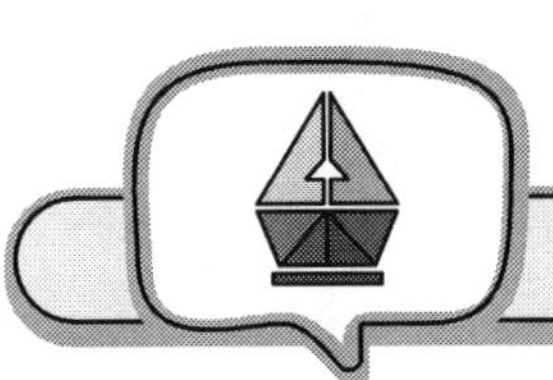

Correcting and Comprehending Sentences

Directions: Read and correct the sentences below. Check each sentence and make sure it has:

* The right homophone
* Proper capitalization
* Verb agreement

1. You're mom bake good Cookies.

____

2. I will eats too of the cookies.

____

3. There really good!

____

4. can She teaches me how two make them?

____

5. I will make them for my aunt kayla.

____

Directions: Answer the questions below about the sentences you read and corrected.

1. Who made the cookies?

   A. Your mom

   B. Me

   C. You

2. How many cookies did the person eat?

   A. Two

   B. Too

   C. Three

3. Who will they make the cookies for?

   A. Your mom

   B. Aunt Kayla

   C. You

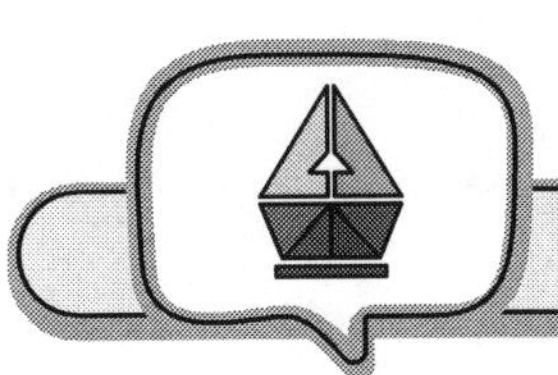

Prefixes and Suffixes

Directions: Read each word. Then, choose what it means.

1. What does the word disappear mean?

   A. appear again

   B. not appear

   C. appear before

2. What does the word warmest mean?

   A. not warm

   B. full of warm

   C. the most warm

3. I got to school ....

   A. safer

   B. safest

   C. safely

4. What would someone who is full of help be called?

   A. helpful

   B. helper

   C. helply

5. What does the word miner mean?

   A. someone who mines

   B. the most mined

   C. not a mine

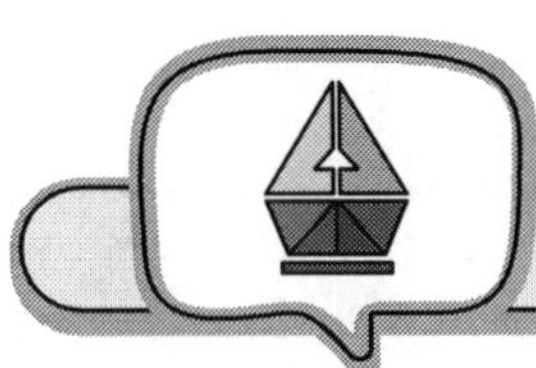

6. What would the most friendly person be called?

   A. friendlier

   B. friendliest

   C. unfriendly

7. What does the word faster mean?

   A. the most fast

   B. more fast

   C. without fast

8. What would it be called if you read a book again?

   A. reread

   B. preread

   C. disread

9. I .... my uncle when I did not look both ways before crossing the street.

   A. disobeyed

   B. preobeyed

   C. obeyer

10. Which word means without end?

   A. endness

   B. ender

   C. endless

Plural Nouns

Directions: Write the correct plural of the word. The rules for pluralizing nouns are below.

1. For most nouns, add an s to the end of the word.

2. If a noun ends in ch, sh, s, x, or z, you add an es.

3. If a noun ends in y, you usually add ies.

4. Keep an eye out for irregular nouns! They don't follow any rules at all.

Singular Noun	Plural Noun	Singular Noun	Plural Noun
child		baby	
dish		glass	
apple		cookie	
butterfly		box	
book		puppy	
fox		bus	
mouse		man	
zebra		brush	
woman		pony	
paper		person	

Spelling Test

In this activity, you will take a quick spelling test.

Directions: Find an adult or a friend to read fifteen of your sight words to you, one word at a time. They can pick any of the words you've learned so far.

When they call out a word, you'll write it on the line. At the end, work together to see how you did.

1.

2.

3.

4.

5.

6.

7.

8.

9.

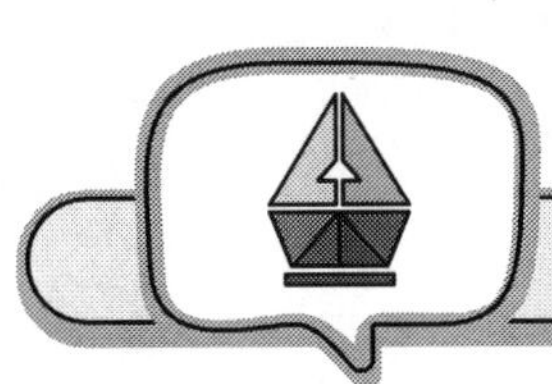

10. ____

11. ____

12. ____

13. ____

14. ____

15. ____

Write an Interesting Sentence

You've learned that every sentence has to have a noun and a verb to make sense, but now you've learned that adjectives and adverbs can make sentences more exciting!

Directions: Rewrite each sentence with an adjective, adverb, or both! An example has been done for you.

1. The balloon floated.

   <u>The red balloon floated high in the sky.</u>

2. She sang a song.

3. The cheetah chased the gazelle.

4. The ice cream melted.

5. The puppy wagged its tail.

6. He read the book.

7. The giraffe stretched its neck to reach the leaves.

8. She smiled when she saw her friends.

9. The bear slept in the cave.

10. The cat purred.

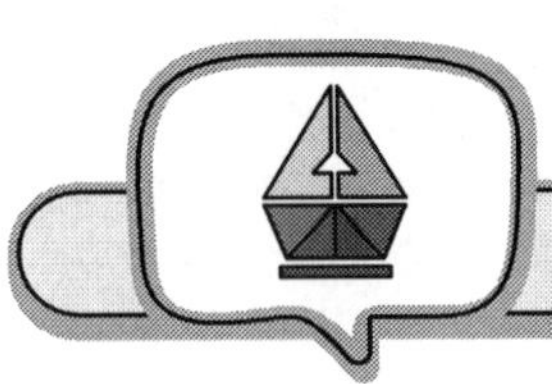

Contractions and Compound Words

Directions: Read each sentence. **Rewrite** the sentence with contractions. Then, **underline** any compound words you see.

An example has been done for you.

1. I am going to the playground.
    I'm going to the <u>playground.</u>

2. I will help you with your homework.

3. We are eating hotdogs.

4. They are having a surprise birthday party for her.

5. She is going to be so excited to see her snowman cake.

6. We will eat cupcakes and have a great time!

WEEK 12

Interrogatives

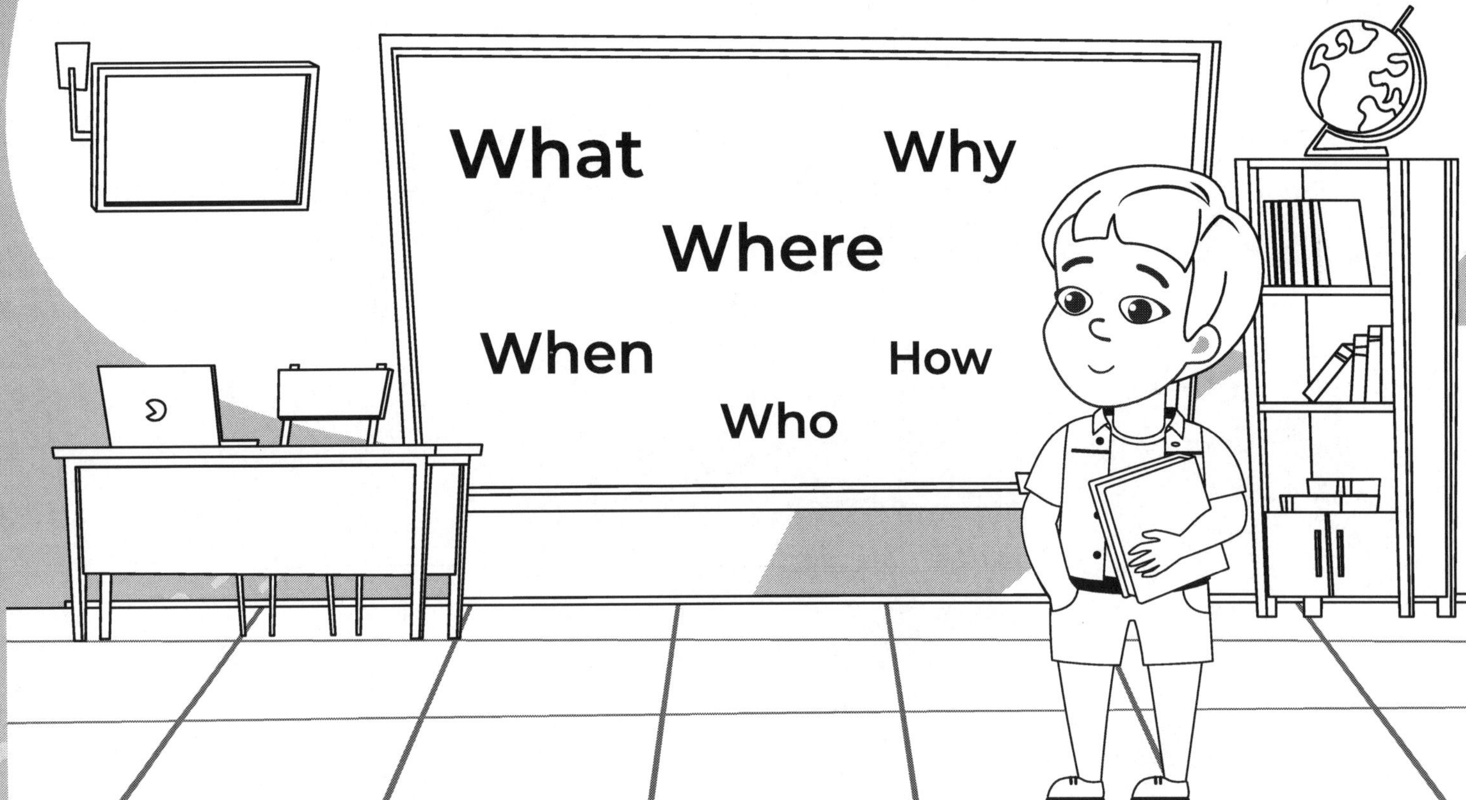

This week you'll learn about a new, special kind of a word called an interrogative! Interrogatives are question words.

Let's get going with the next half of our learning!

This week, you'll be learning about **interrogatives**. Interrogative is a fancy word for question words!

Read the sentences below. Do you see the interrogative sentences?

The sun is shining.

What is your name?

She loves to read.

Where are you going?

The second and fourth sentences were interrogatives! They were asking questions to get more information rather than just telling information. Fun fact: sentences that just tell information are called **declarative** sentences!

Interrogative sentences often begin with the following words:

- Who

- What

- Where

- When

- Why

- How

In the activities on the next few pages, you will practice more with interrogatives.

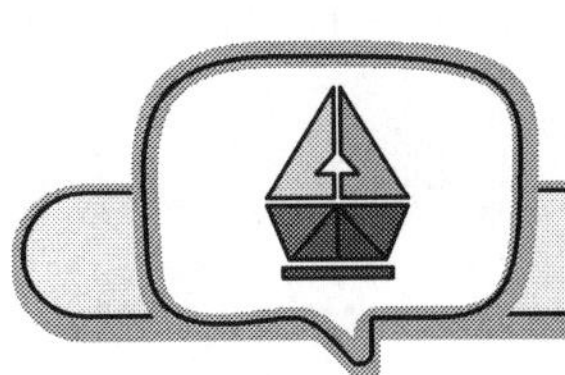

Interrogative Word Search

To identify interrogative sentences, you have to know which words are interrogatives!

Directions: Find the interrogatives in the word search.

Word Search

H	O	W	U	C	C	S	J	Q	M	C	L
L	W	H	A	T	P	H	X	H	C	G	U
K	Z	V	I	K	W	W	H	I	C	H	M
W	C	E	I	D	H	V	F	C	X	M	H
H	T	I	L	S	E	A	W	H	Y	J	G
O	J	Z	H	L	N	Y	X	K	F	M	Q
S	Q	Z	P	R	W	H	E	R	E	D	R
O	T	I	A	A	I	G	B	N	T	S	Q

Directions: Find the following words in the puzzle.

Words are hidden ➡ and ⬇.

HOW	WHEN	WHICH	WHY
WHAT	WHERE	WHO	

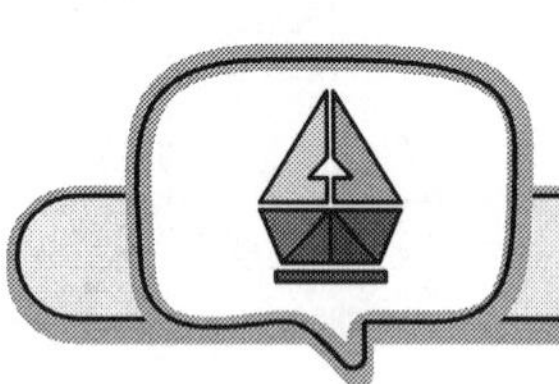

Make it an Interrogative

Directions: Read each sentence. Then, change the sentence into an interrogative. Remember to make sure each sentence ends with a question mark! An example has been done for you.

1. You like ice cream.

<u>Which ice cream do you like?</u>

2. He has a pet cat.

3. I have a best friend.

4. Cats like to chase mice.

5. My favorite color is purple.

6. Elephants are big animals.

7. The flowers are blooming in the garden.

....

8. We play games during recess.

....

9. I have stuffed animals on my bed.

....

10. I like to read stories.

....

Interrogative Quiz

Directions: Fill in the blank with the correct interrogative.

1. .... is your favorite color?

   A. Where   **B.** What   **C.** When

2. .... is your school located?

   A. How   **B.** Which   **C.** Where

3. .... do you go to bed at night?

   A. Who   **B.** What   **C.** When

4. .... is your pet's name?

   A. Where   **B.** What   **C.** Which

5. .... are you feeling today?

   A. What   **B.** Who   **C.** How

6. .... did you visit last summer?

   A. How   **B.** Where   **C.** What

7. .... do you like to eat for breakfast?

   A. What

   B. Which

   C. Who

8. .... is your best friend?

   A. Where

   B. Who

   C. What

9. .... is your favorite subject in school?

   A. Who

   B. What

   C. Why

10. .... do you celebrate your birthday?

   A. How

   B. What

   C. Which

Declarative or Interrogative?

Directions: Read the sentences below. **Write** the proper punctuation at the end of the sentence.

1. I have a blue backpack _

2. How big are elephants _

3. What do you like to do after school _

4. Our school has a big playground _

5. Which ice cream flavor do you like best _

6. Where is your backpack _

7. The sun rises in the east _

8. Where are you going on vacation _

9. My pajamas are yellow _

10. How old is your baby sister _

Now, **write** three interrogative sentences of your own!

1. ____

2. ____

3. ____

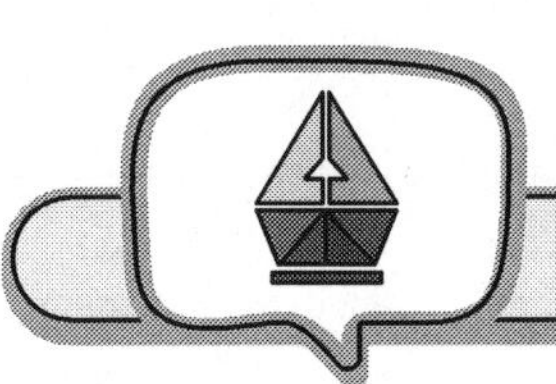

Snap Word Practice

Today we will learn **four** new snap words! With your adult, read the snap words below.

when	went	what	where

Did you notice that your snap words this week were all interrogatives? Write the words in the boxes below.

To learn your new snap words, we'll play a game called **Snap Word Sentences**!

Directions: Use each snap word to **write** a sentence. Be sure to use correct capitalization and punctuation!

Sentence 1 - when

Sentence 2 - went

Sentence 3 - what

Sentence 4 - where

Prepositions

This week, you will learn about another type of special word called a preposition. A preposition helps you understand more about a noun in sentence.

Last week, you learned that interrogatives are question words. This week, you'll learn about another special type of word: prepositions.

A **preposition** is a word that shows what a noun is doing! It tells more about the noun's place, when the noun was doing something, or how it was doing it.

Read the list of prepositions below.

Where Prepositions	When Prepositions	How Prepositions
in	for	to
on	before	from
at	after	into
by	during	through
near	until	along
between	since	across
behind	from	onto
above	to	off
below	throughout	over
beside	within	up

Just like adjectives and adverbs, prepositions can help make our sentences more interesting and provide more details.

In the activities on the next few pages, you will learn more about using prepositions.

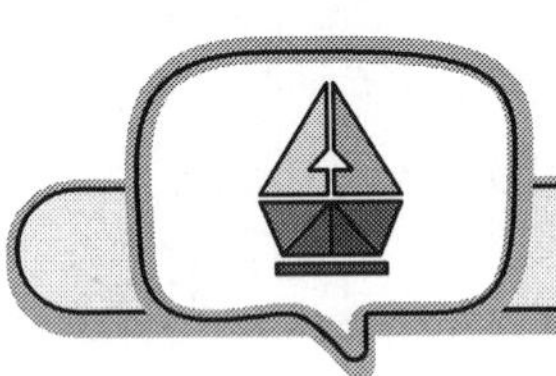

Preposition Word Search

Directions: Find the prepositions in the word search.

Word Search

```
V M V A U N T I L I W D B L T X A Q
F O R T H R O U G H E Q E W H S L J
X S J B E F O R E F R A H P R F O W
B T N S F R O M B P A Z I N O O N K
H Q H W I T H I N L C G N I U D G B
O O V E R E E U L G R P D A G U Z E
F B E T W E E N F N O K E B H R C S
F B W P D I A X R N S E U O O I I I
S Q L S I N C E O V S T A V U N N D
V U Y N E A R G M O P Z L E T G T E
D A F T E R U F F P L B R C J A O O
J E V N B E L O W R K W F M D L K B
```

Directions: Find the following words in the puzzle.

Words are hidden ➔ and ↓.

ABOVE	BEHIND	FOR	ONTO	UNTIL
ACROSS	BELOW	FROM	OVER	WITHIN
AFTER	BESIDE	INTO	SINCE	
ALONG	BETWEEN	NEAR	THROUGH	
BEFORE	DURING	OFF	THROUGHOUT	

Where Prepositions

One thing prepositions can tell us is where a noun is.

Directions: Look at the pictures below. **Write** a sentence with a preposition from the word bank to match the picture. **Underline** the preposition.

An example has been done for you.

Preposition Word Bank: beside, at, below, on, by, between, in, above, behind, near.

	The cat is <u>in</u> the box.

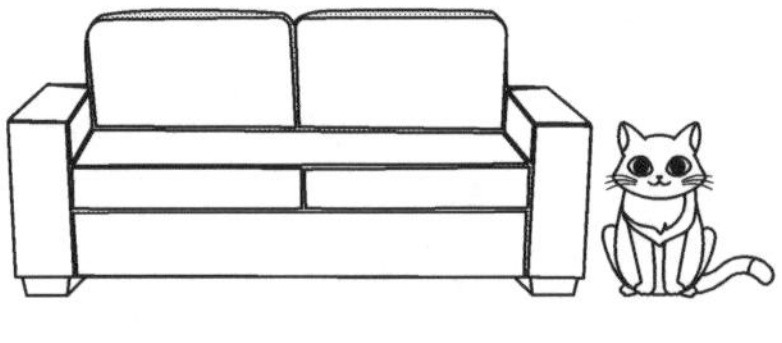	

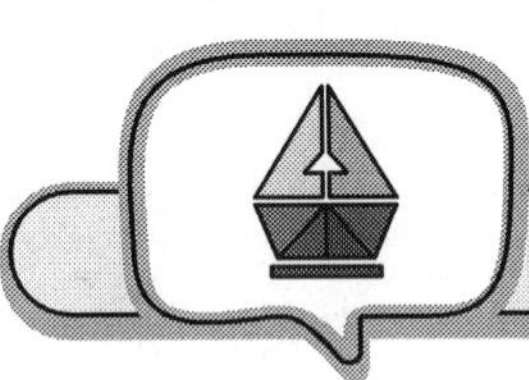

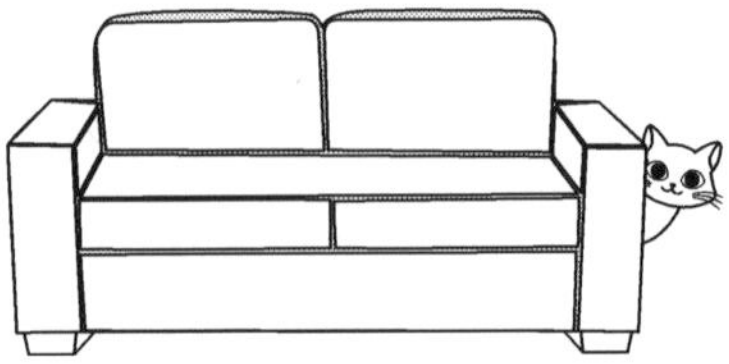

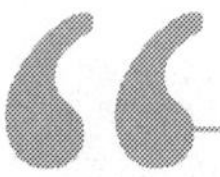

When Prepositions

Prepositions can also tell us when something is happening.

Directions: Use the prompts to **write** a sentence using a when preposition. **Circle** the preposition you use. You can use the word bank to help you. An example has been done for you. Use another piece of paper to write your sentences.

Preposition Word Bank: since, to, in, after, during, until, before.

What is something you do for two minutes?
I brush my teeth for two minutes.

1. What is something you haven't done since last year?

2. What is something you do at night?

3. What is something that happens during the summer?

4. What do you do on your birthday?

5. What do you do in the morning?

6. What do you have to do until you're finished?

7. What do you do before you eat dinner?

8. What do you do after you put your pajamas on?

9. How do you get to school?

How Prepositions

Finally, prepositions can tell us how a noun does something. How prepositions are usually used with verbs.

Directions: Read the sentences below. **Rewrite** each sentence with a how preposition from the word bank. You may use each preposition more than once.

Preposition Word Bank: onto, along, from, to, through, off, up, into, across, over.

1. The elephant runs .... the savannah.

____

2. We drive .... the tunnel.

____

3. She ran .... the finish line.

____

4. We walked back .... the cafeteria.

____

5. They went .... the haunted house.

____

6. The river runs .... the park.

....

7. The trapeze artist walks .... the tightrope.

....

8. I hung .... the monkey bars.

....

9. I jumped .... the swings.

....

10. The bat went .... the chimney.

....

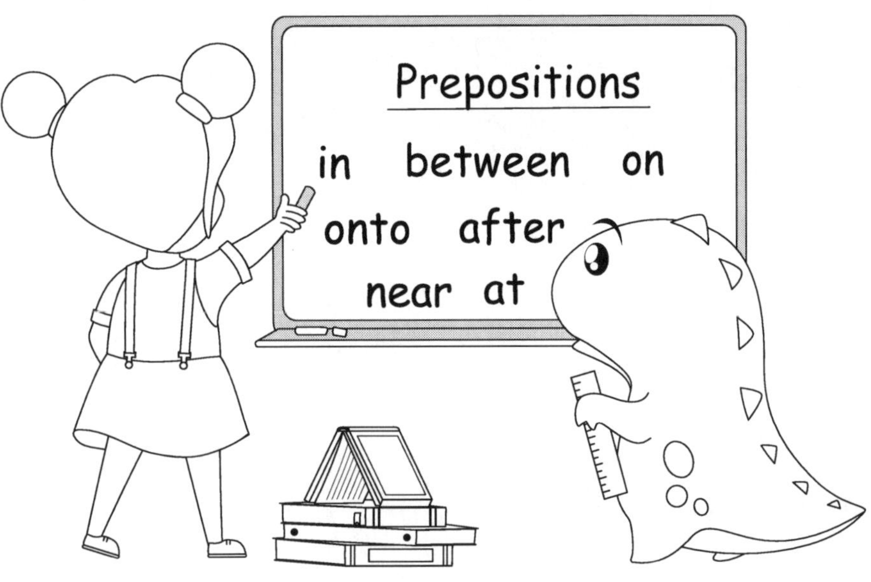

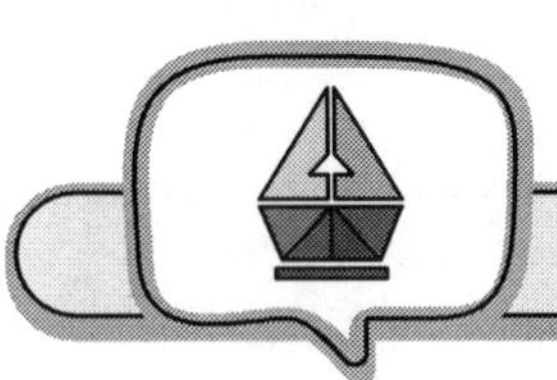 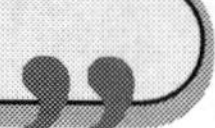

Write Your Own Preposition Sentences.

Directions: Use the list of prepositions below to **write** your own sentences with prepositions. **Underline** the prepositions you use.

Where Prepositions	When Prepositions	How Prepositions
in	for	to
on	before	from
at	after	into
by	during	through
near	until	along
between	since	across
behind	from	onto
above	to	off
below	throughout	over
beside	within	up

1. ____

2. ____

3. ____

4. ____

5. ____

Snap Word Practice

Today we will learn **four** new snap words! With your adult, read the snap words below.

together   several   begin   before

Write the words in the boxes below.

To learn your new snap words, we'll play a game called **Snap Word Timed Write**!

Directions: Set a timer for one minute. Write your word as many times as you can in minute. Then, set the timer again and see if you can write more words!

together	several	begin	before

WEEK 14
Pronouns
yourself
we
they
them
us
himself
him
she
me
her
he
you
I
myself
This week you will learn about pronouns! Pronouns can be helpful when you need a word to take the place of a noun in a sentence.
ARGOPREP

Last week, you learned that a **preposition** is a word that shows what a noun is doing! It tells more about the noun's place, when the noun was doing something, or how it was doing it.

This week, you'll learn about another special type of word: **pronouns**. A **pronoun** is a word that takes the place of a noun.

We don't always need to read the same noun over and over again. **Read** the two short stories below. One has pronouns and one does not. See what you notice about the stories.

* Sherry went to the store. Sherry got apples. Sherry loves apples. Sherry will use the apples to make pie. Sherry will eat the pie with Karly and Lyle.

* Sherry went to the store. She got apples. She loves them! Sherry will use the apples to make pie. She will eat it with her family.

The second story was a little shorter because it replaced the proper noun, Sherry, with "she." A few other pronouns were used, too, but we'll get to that a little later!

There are a few types of pronouns you will learn about and use. **Read** the chart below.

Singular Pronouns	Plural Pronouns	Reflexive Pronouns
I	we	himself
me	they	myself
you	them	herself
her	us	yourself
him		itself
she		ourselves
he		themselves
it		

In the activities on the next few pages, you will learn more about using pronouns to replace nouns.

Singular Pronouns

Singular pronouns are pronouns that take the place of singular nouns. Singular pronouns refer to just one person, place, or thing.

Read the examples of singular pronouns below.

I, me, you, her, him, she, he, it

Now, **read** the sentences below. **Rewrite** the sentence and replace the underlined noun with a pronoun from the list above.

1. <u>The present</u> was wrapped in gold wrapping paper.

....

2. <u>Yvonne</u> gave the present to <u>Billy</u>.

....

3. <u>Billy</u> loved <u>the present</u>.

....

4. <u>Yvonne's</u> mom got the present from the store.

....

5. <u>Billy's sister</u> liked the present, too.

....

Plural Pronouns

Plural pronouns are pronouns that take the place of plural nouns. Plural pronouns refer to more than one person, place, or thing.

Read the examples of plural pronouns below.

we, they, them, us

Sometimes it can be hard to decide if you should use a singular pronoun or a plural pronoun. You may have to think about what makes sense and try it a few times.

Directions: Read the sentences below. **Rewrite** each sentence, and replace the underlined nouns with pronouns.

1. <u>Sam and I</u> ate a lot of candy.

2. <u>My friends</u> gave me cards.

3. I made cards for <u>my classmates.</u>

4. <u>My dad</u> made cupcakes for my class.

5. <u>My sister's</u> teddy bear has a heart on it.

Reflexive Pronouns

A reflexive pronoun refers back to a person or thing. It is easiest to understand reflexive pronouns in sentences.

Read the examples of each reflexive pronoun in a sentence.

He gave himself a hug.

I can tie my shoes by myself.

She washed herself before dinner.

You should be proud of yourself.

The cat groomed itself on the couch.

We need to take care of ourselves.

They enjoyed the movie all by themselves.

Directions: In each sentence, **look** at the underlined word and circle whether it refers to the same person or thing mentioned earlier in the sentence.

Hint: Check to see if you could replace the underlined word with a reflexive pronoun. It might require you to rewrite the sentence.

I can tie <u>my own</u> shoes.

Refers to: (Myself/Someone else)

1. She made a sandwich for <u>Makayla</u>.

    Refers to: (Herself/Someone else)

2. They cleaned the house for <u>their grandma</u>.

Refers to: (Themselves/Someone else)

3. He talked to <u>his reflection</u> in the mirror.

Refers to: (Himself/Someone else)

4. We cooked dinner <u>alone</u>.

Refers to: (Ourselves/Someone else)

5. The dog groomed <u>his paw</u>.

Refers to: (Itself/Someone else)

6. Do you believe in you?

Refers to: (Yourself/Someone else)

7. After the game, the players congratulated <u>their team</u>.

Refers to: (Themselves/Someone else)

8. She watched the TV show <u>alone</u>.

Refers to: (Herself/Someone else)

9. He bought a new suit for <u>his closet</u>.

Refers to: (Himself/Someone else)

Using Pronouns

Directions: Read the sentences, **write** the correct pronoun from the word bank in the blank. You will use some pronouns more than once.

Word Bank: he, she, it, we, they, you

1. Sarah is my friend. .... likes to read books.

2. Tom and Mary are playing outside. .... are having fun.

3. The cat is chasing a mouse. .... is very fast.

4. Mom and Dad are making dinner. .... are making spaghetti.

5. Sam and I went to the park. .... played on the swings.

6. Lisa is singing a song. .... has a beautiful voice.

7. The dogs are barking. .... want to go for a walk.

8. You can ride your bike. .... can go to the park.

Directions: Write the correct pronoun in the blank.

1. Sarah and .... went to the store.

   A. I

   B. she

   C. they

2. .... wagged its tail happily.

   A. It

   B. Its

   C. Them

3. .... can play the piano very well.

    A. We

    B. Us

    C. Him

4. I like to ride my bike, and .... do too.

    A. they

    B. them

    C. I

5. Tim and .... built a sandcastle at the beach.

    A. he

    B. his

    C. I

Write Your Own Pronoun Sentences

Directions: Use the list of pronouns below to **write** your own sentences with prounouns. **Underline** the prepositions you use. Be sure to use at least one pronoun of each type.

Singular Pronouns	Plural Pronouns	Reflexive Pronouns
I	we	himself
me	they	myself
you	them	herself
her	us	yourself
him		itself
she		ourselves
he		themselves
it		

1. ____

2. ____

3. ____

4. ____

5. ____

Snap Word Practice

Today we will learn **four** new snap words! With your adult, read the snap words below.

themselves   either   while   everybody

Write the words in the boxes below.

To learn your new snap words, we'll play a game called **Snap Word Bingo!**

Directions: Have an adult or friend call out snap words from the bingo card below. When you get five snap words in a row, call out "bingo!"

better	everybody	when	outside	happen
begin	trouble	question	beautiful	great
slowly	several	themselves	follow	very
where	different	special	what	suddenly
either	does	together	probably	while

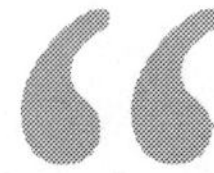

Before you go, review your snap words. If you find one you don't know, **circle** it so you know which words you need to practice!

better	follow	happen	different	very
somewhere	anyone	nobody	outside	question
slowly	suddenly	probably	usually	answer
goes	does	begin	trouble	special
great	excited	beautiful	old	when
went	what	where	together	several
begin	before	themselves	either	while
everybody				

WEEK 15

Commas

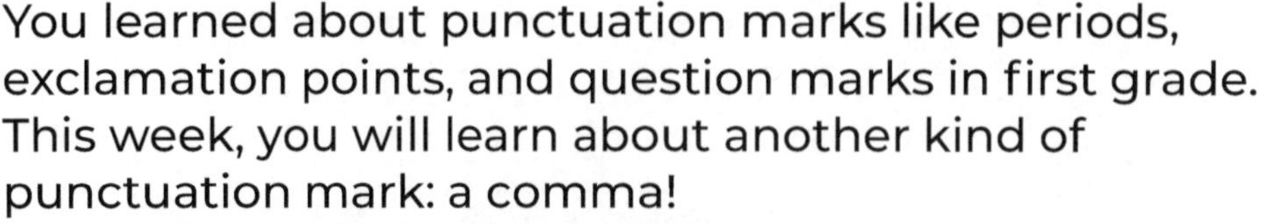

You learned about punctuation marks like periods, exclamation points, and question marks in first grade. This week, you will learn about another kind of punctuation mark: a comma!

Last week, you learned that a **pronoun** is a word that takes the place of a noun.

This week, you'll learn about **commas**. A comma is a punctuation mark, like a period or a question mark, but it doesn't come at the end of a sentence.

Commas look like this **,**

In second grade, you have a few places you want to make sure you use commas.

Read the chart below with your adult to learn when and how to use commas

Commas in dates

April 27, 2016
June 25, 2011

★ **The comma goes between the day and year!**

Commas in a series

I like pink, blue, and yellow.

I went with Jared, Harper, and Gibson.

★ **Put commas after words that are part of a series or list and have 3 or more words.**

Commas in friendly letters

Oct. 10, 2022
Dear Andry,
  Thanks for coming to my party. I loved the gift you got for me. You are a great friend!
Love, Layne

★ **The comma goes in the date, after the greeting, and after the closing**

Commas in cites and states

Tulsa, Oklahoma,
Portland, Oregon
Austin, Texas
San Diego, California

★ **The comma goes between the city and the state.**

In the activities on the next few pages, you will learn more about when and how to use commas.

Commas in Dates

Commas are used when writing dates. The comma goes between the day and the year.

February 3, 2000

Directions: Write a comma in the dates below.

1. January 10 2023

2. March 25 2023

3. May 6 2023

4. July 14 2023

5. September 3 2023

6. November 22 2023

7. February 8 2023

8. April 30 2023

9. June 12 2023

10. August 29 2023

Use the line below to write the date of your next birthday with a comma.

Commas in a Letter

We also use commas when writing a letter. A typical friendly letter looks like this. Pay attention to the arrows to see all of the commas. How many do you count?

July 1, 2023

Dear Malik,

I hope you are having fun on vacation! I hope you get to swim with dolphins. I can't wait to see you when you get back.

Love,
Sophie

This example shows the places commas are always used in a friendly letter. They are:

* In the date at the top of the letter

* After the opening statement (Dear Malik,)

* After the closing statement (Love,)

Directions: On the lines below, pretend to be Malik and **write** a letter to Sophie, telling her about your vacation. Be sure to include commas in the correct places.

Commas in a List

The last place you will want to be on the lookout for commas in second grade is in a list! Commas are used in lists to help make the list easier to read.

Read the sentence below and see what you notice.

> When we went to the store, we got grapes apples bananas chicken nuggets cheese bread and snacks.

That sentence is pretty hard to read! Adding commas in lists that have more than three items helps us read long lists. Let's read that example sentence again, but this time with commas.

> When we went to the store, we got grapes, apples, bananas, chicken nuggets, cheese, bread, and snacks.

Much better!

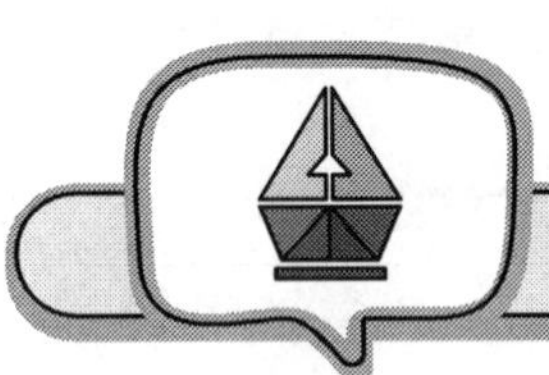

Directions: Read the list of words below. Then, **write** a sentence with every item in the list, separated by commas.

Example: red   blue   green

My favorite colors are red, blue, and green.

1	cereal	milk	toast
2	lions	tigers	bears
3	flowers	vegetables	fruits
4	swim	play	run
5	swing	slide	climb

1.

2.

3.

4.

5.

Letter with a List

Directions: Use the space below to **write** a friendly letter to someone. In your letter, use at least one list that must be separated by commas.

Date: ....

Comma Quiz

Directions: Read each sentence below. Then, add commas where they belong.

1. I have a cat dog and a fish as pets.

2. November 7 2017

3. Yesterday I went to the park with my friends Sarah Jake and Tim.

4. June 14 2024

5. In the forest we saw squirrels birds and rabbits.

6. My mom asked me to clean my room sweep the floor and make my bed.

7. I love to draw paint and color with crayons.

8. On my birthday I got a new bike a soccer ball and a kite.

9. At the store I want to buy apples bananas and oranges.

10. September 8 2022

Snap Word Practice

Today we will learn **four** new snap words! With your adult, read the snap words below.

enough   again   being   ready

Write the words in the boxes below.

To learn your new snap words, we'll play a game called **Hat Draw Write!**

Directions: Write the numbers 1-4 on pieces of paper. Then, put the pieces of paper into a hat. Draw a number out of the hat, and write the word it corresponds to.

For example, if you draw a 3 out of the hat, write the word "being" in the correct column.

1- enough	2 - again	3 - being	4 - ready

Conjunctions

For

And

But

Or

Yet

So

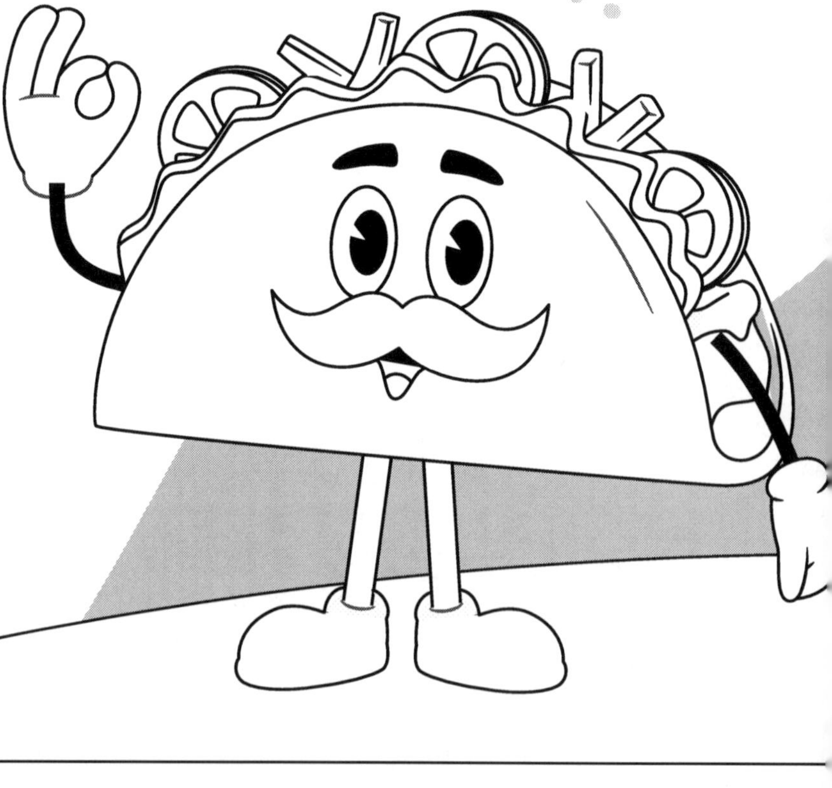

This week, you will add to your knowledge about special types of words by learning about conjunctions!

Week 16 Conjunctions

Last week, you learned that a comma is a punctuation mark, like a period or a question mark, but it doesn't come at the end of a sentence. Commas are used in dates, friendly letters, and in lists.

This week, you'll learn about **conjunctions**. Conjunctions are words that connect sentences together. To remember your conjunctions, you can use the word fanboys!

F - for

A - and

N - nor

B - but

O - or

Y - yet

S - so

Coordinating Conjunctions:

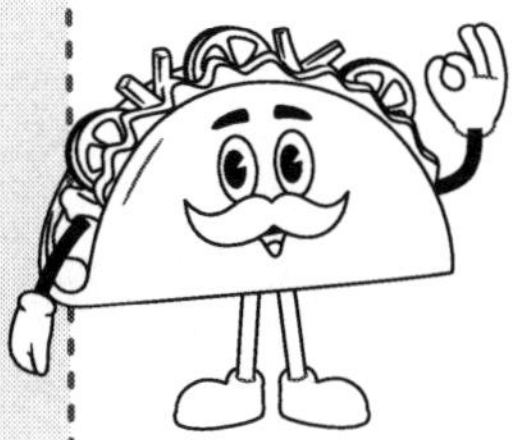

connects 2 independent clauses!

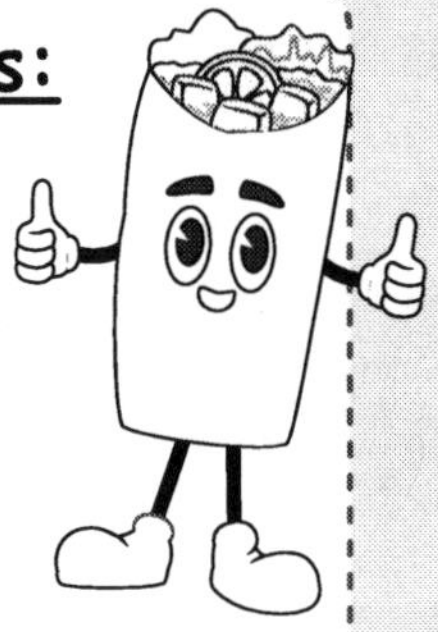

For	~	Today I ate 6 tacos, **for** I was so hungry!
And	~	I like my burrito with rice **and** cheese.
Nor	~	He doesn't like burritos, **nor** does he like tacos.
But	~	The store was out of burritos, **but** they had tacos!
Or	~	Would you rather have a crunchy burrito, **or** a soft taco?
Yet	~	Some tacos can be really spicy, **yet** so yummy!
So	~	I was starving, **so** I had a chicken and a steak burrito.

In the activities on the next few pages, you will learn more about when and how to use conjunctions.

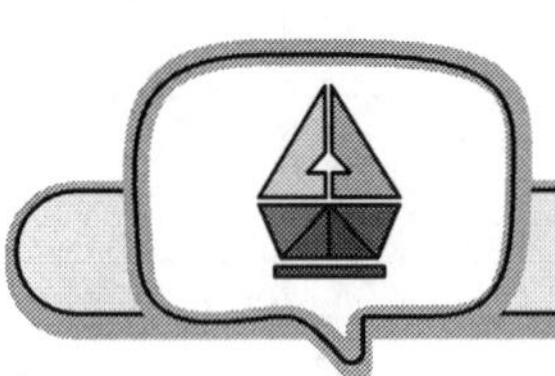

Conjunction Maze

Directions: Guide the dog back to his dog house. Start at the top and follow and shade in the boxes with conjunction words from the word bank.

Word Bank: for, and, nor, but, or, yet, so

so	quickly	she
nor	or	before
too	yet	where
for	but	above
and	under	what
nor	so	and

You should have shaded in ten boxes. **Write** the conjunction from each box.

1. so

2.

3.

4.

5.

6.

7.

8.

9.

10.

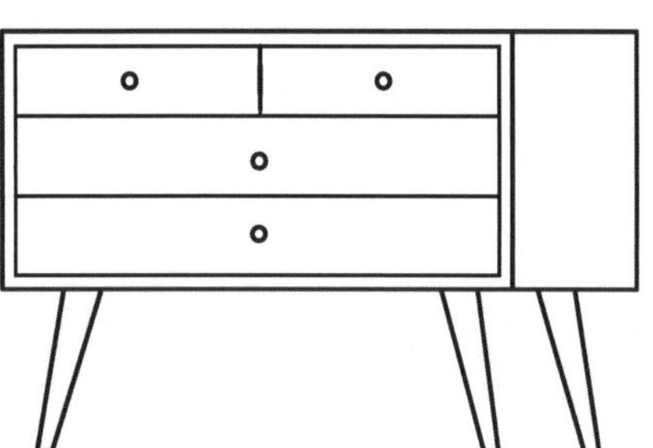

Conjunction Word Search

Directions: Find the conjunctions in the word search!

```
K  L  Q  P  V  P  P  J  T  E  K  F
W  Y  F  T  W  G  F  G  R  G  S  P
I  E  Y  B  U  T  U  A  V  L  Y  F
V  T  C  E  W  F  R  X  A  N  D  F
B  A  C  X  K  S  V  V  Y  I  G  O
F  A  I  I  A  O  N  O  R  S  U  R
B  Q  M  E  E  S  L  Z  Y  F  Y  B
D  G  J  U  O  R  A  N  O  Y  D  B
```

Directions: Find the following words in the puzzle.

Words are hidden ➡ and ⬇.

AND	OR
BUT	SO
FOR	YET
NOR	

And, But, Or

The conjunctions you will use the most often are **and, but,** and **or**.

Directions: Read the sentences below. Use the correct conjunction (and, but, or) to join the two sentences together to make a new sentence. Write the new sentence on the lines provided.

1. The sun is shining. The birds are singing.

New Sentence: _______________________________

2. I want to play soccer. My friend wants to play basketball.

New Sentence: _______________________________

3. It's raining outside. We can stay indoors and play games.

New Sentence: _______________________________

4. Sarah loves to read. She doesn't like math.

New Sentence: _______________________________

5. You can have a cookie. You can have some fruit.

New Sentence: _______________________________

6. My dog barks loudly. He is very friendly.

New Sentence: ___________________________________

7. I like pizza. I like hamburgers.

New Sentence: ___________________________________

8. We can go to the park. We can visit the zoo.

New Sentence: ___________________________________

9. The cat is black. The dog is brown.

New Sentence: ___________________________________

10. I want to watch a movie. I want to read a book.

New Sentence: ___________________________________

For, Nor, Yet, So

You will only use **for, nor, yet,** and **so** sometimes, but it is still important to recognize and practice them!

Directions: Read the sentences below. Fill in the blanks with the appropriate conjunction ("for," "nor," "yet," or "so") to complete the sentence correctly.

1. She wanted to go to the zoo, ... her little brother preferred the museum.

2. It was raining heavily, ... we decided to stay indoors and play games.

3. John wanted to ride his bike, ... he had to finish his homework first.

4. I don't like pizza, ... I ordered a burger.

5. The car wouldn't start, ... they had to call a tow truck.

6. Emma was neither a vegetarian .... a vegan; she ate meat occasionally.

7. It was getting late, ... we decided to leave the party.

8. He hadn't studied for the test, ... he was worried about his performance.

9. I wanted to go swimming, ... my friend wanted to go hiking in the mountains.

10. The sun was shining brightly, ... everyone was in a cheerful mood.

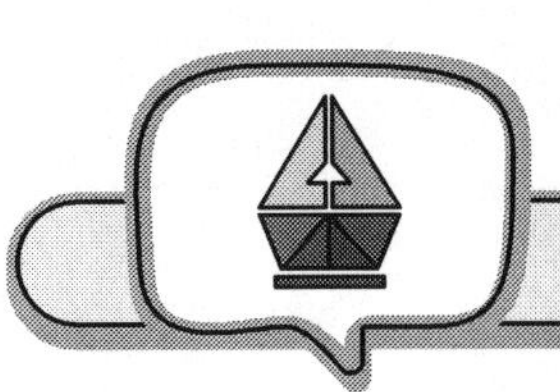 

Snap Word Practice

Today we will learn **four** new snap words! With your adult, read the snap words below.

sometimes   understand   with   against

Write the words in the boxes below.

To learn your new snap words, we'll play a game called **Snap Word Sentences**!

Directions: Use each snap word to **write** a sentence. Be sure to use correct capitalization and punctuation!

Sentence 1 - sometimes

Sentence 2 - understand

Sentence 3 - with

Sentence 4 - against

This week you will learn about simple and compound sentences. By being able to recognize and write each type of sentence, you will be able to make your writing more interesting!

In the last two weeks, you've learned about **commas** and **conjunctions**.

This week, you'll put that knowledge together to create **compound sentences**. A compound sentence is a sentence with two **simple sentences** inside it. A **simple sentence** shows one complete thought.

With **compound sentences**, instead of two separate sentences, you can make one longer sentence by using a **comma** and a **conjunction**.

> (Simple sentence) + (conjunction) + (Simple sentence) = (Compound sentence)

Read the example sentences below.

I should go to school. I am sick.

I should go to school, but I am sick.

Did you see the comma and the conjunction, "but" in the second sentence?

In the activities on the next few pages, you will get more practice with identifying and writing compound sentences.

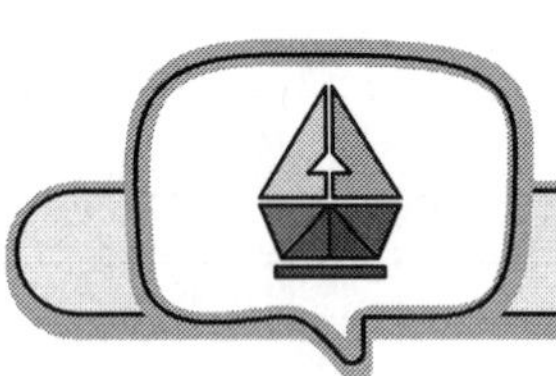

Commas in Compound Sentences

Just like when you used commas in a list, using commas in compound sentences makes them easier to read.

When you are making a compound sentence, you must put a comma before the conjunction.

Look at the example below.

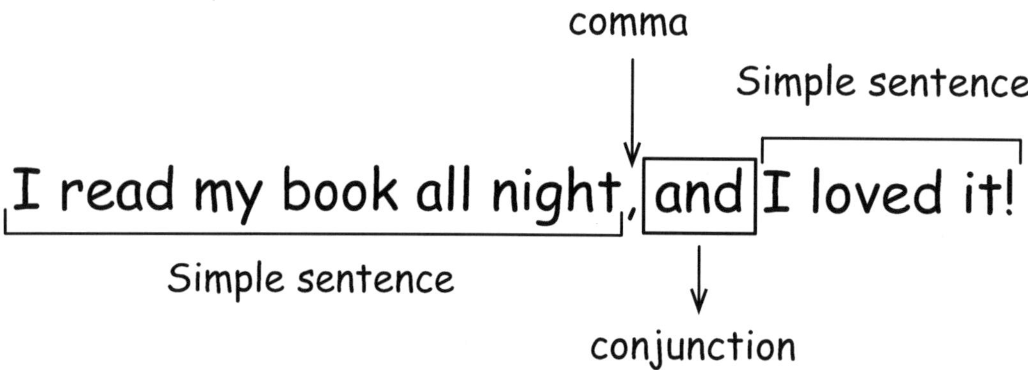

Directions: **Rewrite** each sentence with a comma before the conjunction. **Draw a box** around the conjunction.

1. I like to read books and I like to play soccer.

____

2. Sarah is my best friend and we play together every day.

____

3. The sun is shining and the birds are singing.

____

4. It's raining outside so we can splash in the puddles.

5. Tom wants to go to the beach or he wants to visit the zoo.

6. My dog is small but my cat is big.

7. I like pizza but I like tacos, too.

8. We can go to the park or we can go to the lake.

9. The mouse is fast and it wants cheese.

10. I want to watch a movie or I want to read a book.

Is it a Compound Sentence?

Directions: Read each sentence carefully. Decide whether each sentence is a compound sentence or not. If the sentence is a compound sentence, write "CS" for Compound Sentence. If it is not a compound sentence, write "NS" for Not a Compound Sentence.

1. Mary loves to read books and play basketball. ....

2. The sun was shining, and the sky was clear. ....

3. Dogs are friendly, but cats are independent. ....

4. We can swim in the lake, or we wade in the river. ....

5. She wanted ice cream, but her brother preferred cake. ....

6. He didn't study for the test and was worried about it. ....

7. The weather is nice, yet we decided to stay home. ....

8. My favorite colors are blue and green. ....

9. I like to dance and sing. ....

10. Neither the cat nor the dog wanted to go outside. ....

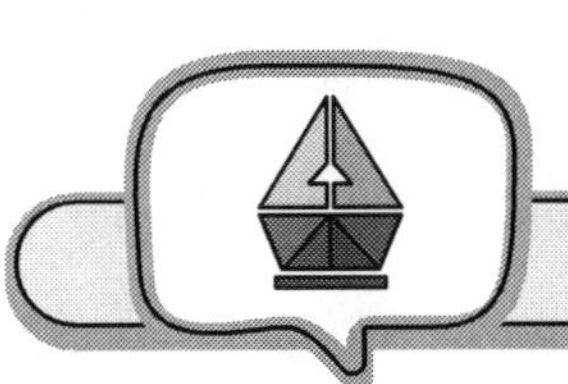

Creating Compound Sentences

Directions: Use the conjunction word bank and a comma to write new compound sentences.

Conjunction Word Bank: for, and, nor, but, or, yet, so

Example:

The three bears wanted to eat.	Their porridge was too hot.

The three bears wanted to eat, but their porridge was too hot.

Greg tried his best.	He fell off his bike.

She was happy to see her aunt.	She squealed in delight.

You can have a peanut butter sandwich.	You can have a turkey sandwich.

I had a bad cold.	I am much better now.

The bakery didn't have any cupcakes left.	They didn't have any fresh bread for sale.

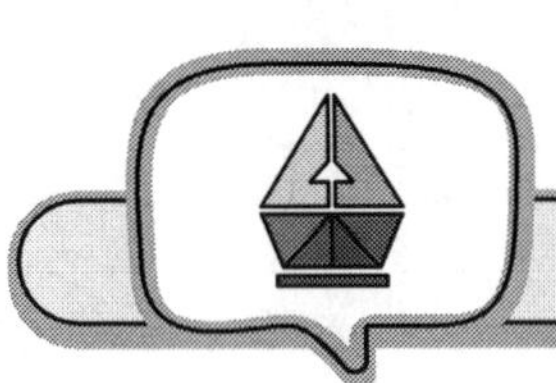

Circle and Write the Conjunction

1. I wanted to go to the park but/or/and I wanted to play video games.

2. She is not a fan of ice cream so/nor/yet she loves frozen yogurt.

3. We can watch a movie or/and/yet we can go for a bike ride.

4. Tom didn't like the pizza but/so/or he ate it anyway.

5. I need to study for the test but/so/nor then I can go to the party.

6. Neither my brother nor/so/for my sister enjoys swimming.

7. Bears can be black but/and/so bears can be other colors.

8. We can go to the zoo yet/and/or we can visit the park.

9. Shanika wanted to play soccer so/nor/but her friend wanted to play basketball.

10. It's raining outside and/but/or we can have fun indoors.

Learning New Snap Words

Today we will learn **three** new snap words! With your adult, read the snap words below.

| terrible | through | excited |

Write the words in the boxes below.

To learn your new snap words, we'll play a game called **Snap Word Pyramid Write!**

Directions: Write one letter of your snap words at a time to make a pyramid.

Example:

h
he
her
here

terrible	through	excited

Collective Nouns

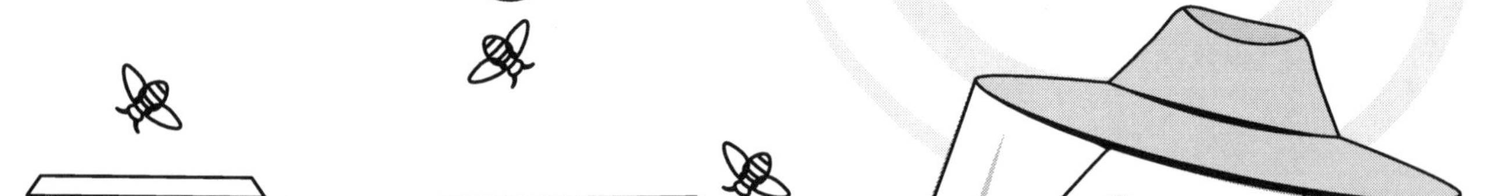

This week, you will learn about collective nouns! Collective nouns are special types of nouns that refer to groups of nouns.

Last week, you learned to create **compound sentences**, by using a comma and a **conjunction**.

This week, you'll learn about collective nouns. A **collective noun** describes a whole group of people, animals, or things.

Read the chart below. The collective noun is underlined.

People	Animals	Things
A <u>crowd</u> of people	A <u>litter</u> of puppies	A <u>bouquet</u> of flowers
A <u>team</u> of players	A <u>school</u> of fish	A <u>fleet</u> of ships
A <u>class</u> of students	An <u>army</u> of ants	A <u>cluster</u> of grapes

There are lots of collective nouns, and you'll learn more of them as you become a stronger reader and writer. Sometimes, you may need to do a bit of research to learn them!

In the activities on the next few pages, you will learn more about collective nouns and how to tell them apart from other types of words.

Learning a Few Collective Nouns

The more you read and write, the more collective nouns you'll learn!

Directions: Read the examples of collective nouns below. Use the boxes to **draw a** picture of the collective noun. Then, **write** a sentence using the collective noun.

Herd of sheep	Colony of ants	Pod of dolphins
Swarm of bees	Crew of people working together on a task	Audience of people
Bunch of bananas	Pack of wolves	Deck of cards

A range of mountains

The mountain range appeared in the distance as we drove down the highway.

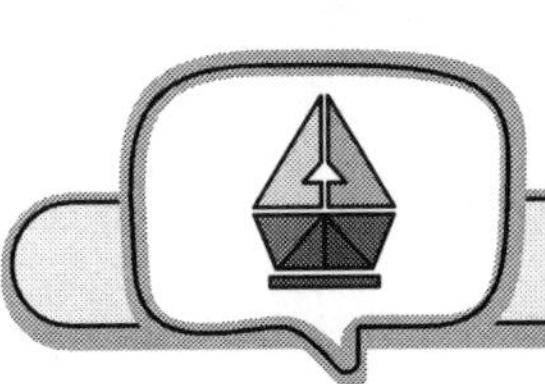

Collective Noun:	Collective Noun:
Picture	Picture
Sentence:	Sentence:

Collective Noun:	Collective Noun:
Picture	Picture
Sentence:	Sentence:

Is it a collective noun?

Learning the different collective nouns will take practice, but one way you can get started is to make sure you can tell the difference between a collective noun and other types of words!

Remember, a **collective noun** is a type of word used to refer to a group of people, things, or animals.

Common noun - a noun that refers to any person, place, or thing

Proper noun - a noun that refers to a specific person, place, or thing; it is always capitalized

Possessive noun - a noun used to show ownership; an apostrophe and an s is added to these nouns

Plural noun - a noun used to refer to more than of a person, place, or thing

Adjective - a word that describes a noun

Adverb - a word that describes a verb

Pronoun - a word used in place of a noun

Verb - an action word that tells what a noun is doing

Directions: Read the words below. In the blanks, write what type of word it is using the list above. Some examples have been done for you.

Flock: <u>collective noun</u>
Running: <u>verb</u>
Sad: <u>adjective</u>

1. Herd: ....

2. Jumping: ....

3. School: ....

4. Fast: ....

5. Team: ....

6. Beautiful: ....

7. Pack: ....

8. Colorful : ....

9. Colony: ....

10. Happy : ....

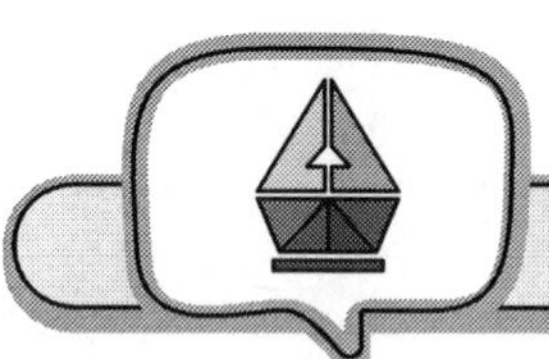

Finding the Collective Nouns

Directions: Read the sentences below. **Underline** the collective noun in each sentence. Then, **write** a short story using the collective noun from one of the sentences.

1. The herd of cows was grazing in the field.

2. I saw a flock of birds flying in the sky.

3. The team of players won the soccer game.

4. We went to watch a school of fish at the aquarium.

5. A pack of wolves howled in the distance.

6. The swarm of bees buzzed around the hive.

7. She picked a bunch of colorful flowers from the garden.

8. The colony of ants worked together to build their nest.

9. A fleet of ships sailed into the harbor.

10. The troop of scouts went on a camping trip.

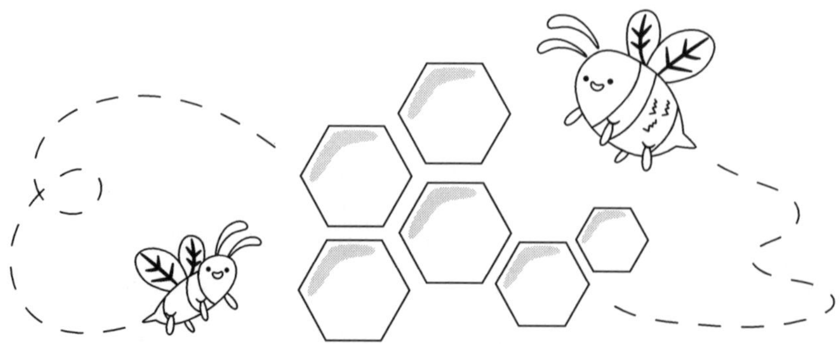

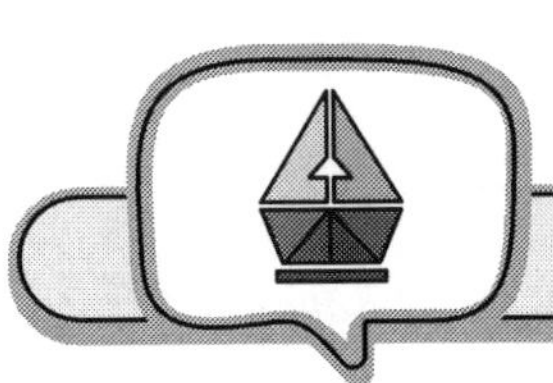

Collective Noun Match

Now that you've learned a few collective nouns, you can think about which collective nouns would make sense with other nouns.

Directions: Match each collective noun to its correct noun. Then, **write** three sentences with the collective nouns from this activity.

A herd of	fish
A pack of	wolves
A team of	bees
A school of	cows
A flock of	players
A swarm of	birds
A colony of	ants
A fleet of	ships
A troop of	scouts
A party of	people

1. ____

2. ____

3. ____

Funny Collective Nouns

Most collective nouns are used for lots of nouns, like **herd**. The collective noun for sheep, cows, elephants, deer, and wildebeest is "herd".

However, some animals have funny names as their collective nouns! You probably won't use these very often in your reading or your writing, but they are fun to know, and you can probably impress your friends and family by knowing them.

Directions: Read the list of funny animal collective nouns below. Choose four, and **draw** a picture of them. Then, **write** a sentence using the collective noun.

1. A murder of crows

2. A crash of rhinoceroses

3. An embarrassment of pandas

4. A business of ferrets

5. A thunder of hippos

6. A crash of jellyfish

7. A flamboyance of flamingos

8. A clowder of cats

9. A knot of toads

10. A prickle of porcupines

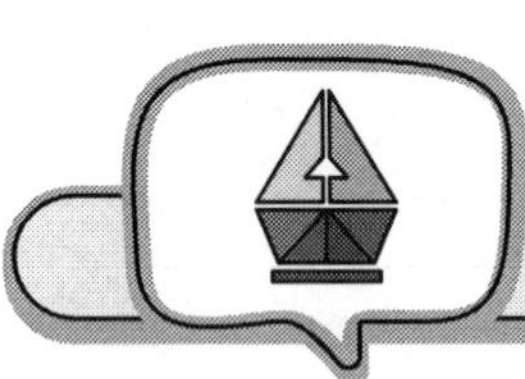

Collective Noun:	Collective Noun:
Picture	Picture
Sentence:	Sentence:
Collective Noun:	Collective Noun:
Picture	Picture
Sentence:	Sentence:

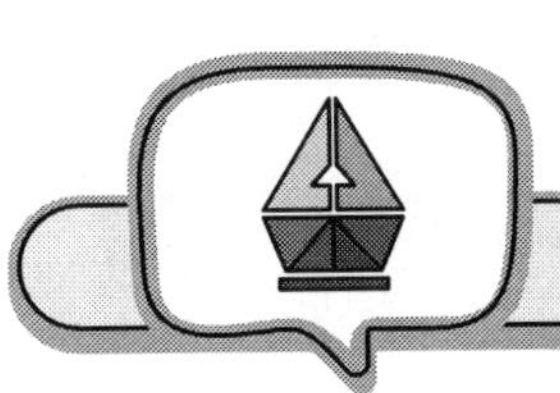

Snap Word Practice

Today we will learn **four** new snap words! With your adult, read the snap words below.

everything   about   bare   bear

Write the words in the boxes below.

To learn your new snap words, we'll play a game called **Snap Word Sentences**!

Directions: Use each snap word to **write** a sentence. Be sure to use correct capitalization and punctuation!

Sentence 1 - everything

Sentence 2 - about

Sentence 3 - bare

Sentence 4 - bear

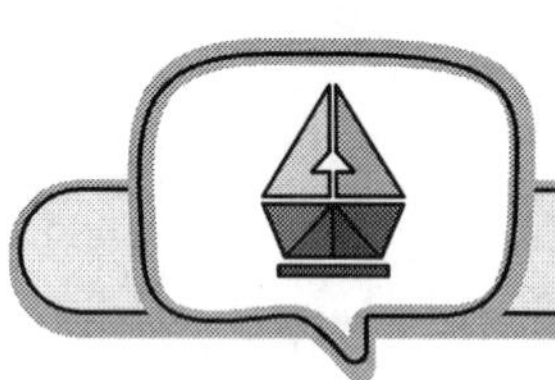

Before you go, review your snap words. If you find one you don't know, **circle** it so you know which words you need to practice!

better	follow	happen	different	very
somewhere	anyone	nobody	outside	question
slowly	suddenly	probably	usually	answer
goes	does	begin	trouble	special
great	excited	beautiful	old	when
went	what	where	together	several
begin	before	themselves	either	while
everybody	enough	again	being	ready
sometimes	understand	with	against	terrible
through	excited	everything	about	bare
bear				

Proofreading and Spelling Strategies

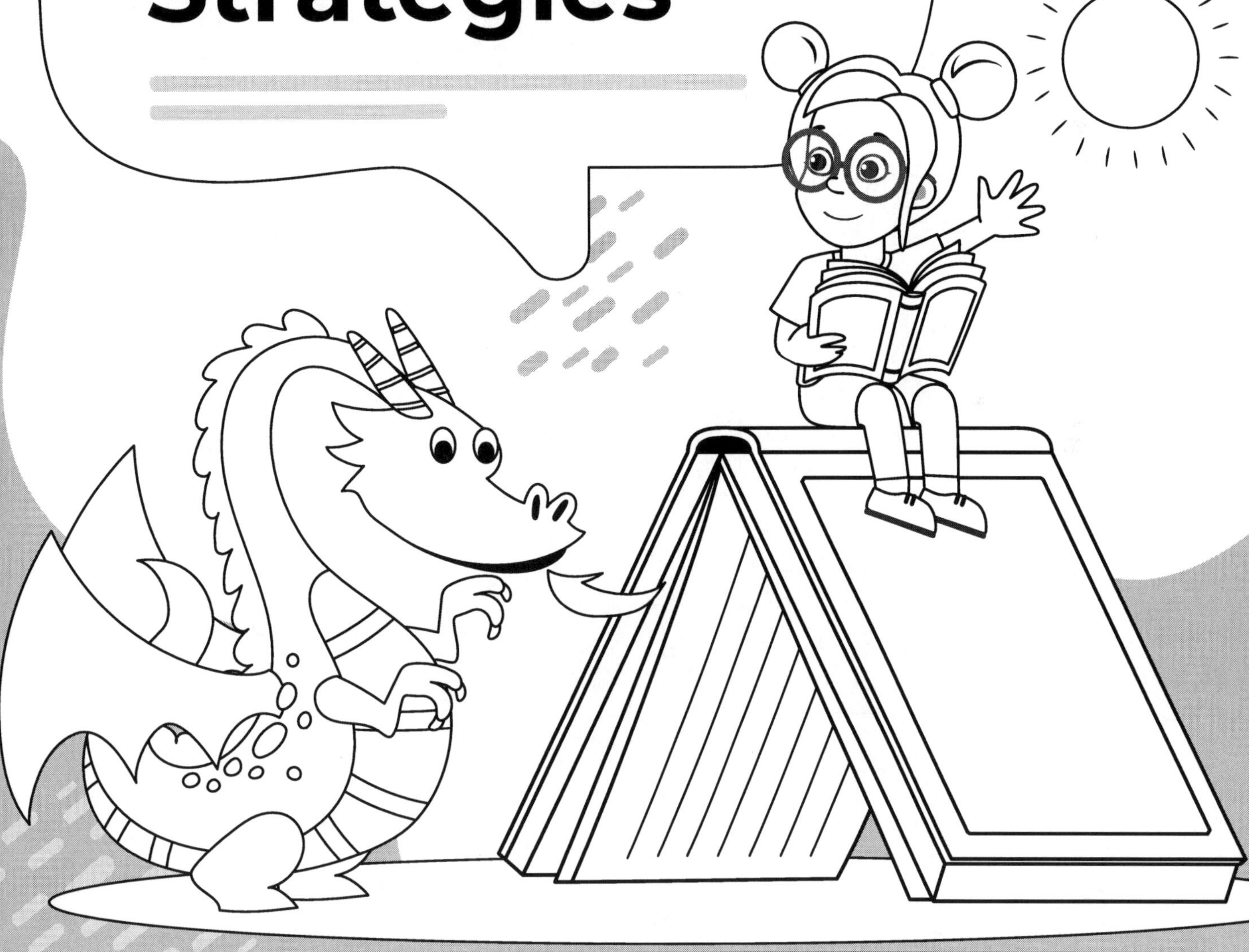

To wrap up your second grade learning, you'll learn some strategies this week for making your writing the very best it can be!

In first grade, you learned a lot about how words are written and the best ways to read them.

In second grade, you've been working hard to learn about types of words and how to make your writing more interesting. Before you review your second grade learning, let's take a week to talk about some proofreading and spelling strategies to help make your writing the best it can be.

In the activities on the next few pages, you will get more practice with proofreading and spelling strategies.

CUPS

Proofreading means checking your writing to make sure it is the best it can be. One way you can proofread your writing is by thinking about cups!

C - capitalization

* Beginning of sentences
* Titles
* Names
* I
* Months

U - usage (verb agreement)

* Make it make sense!

P - punctuation

* Use periods, question marks, and exclamation points to end a sentence
* Use commas in lists
* Use apostrophes to show ownership or in contractions

S - spelling

* Check your words
* Use dictionaries and your list of snap words to help you

Directions: Read the piece of writing below. It has several errors you need to correct. **Rewrite** the writing with correct capitalization, verb agreement, punctuation, and spelling.

One sunny day, lucy and her friend tommy goed to the park They bringed him frisbees, and sokur ball, and play for hours. Lucys mom packed a picnic with sandwich fruit and chips. They ate it under a big oak tree. Lucy said, "I cant believe what a grate day we had"

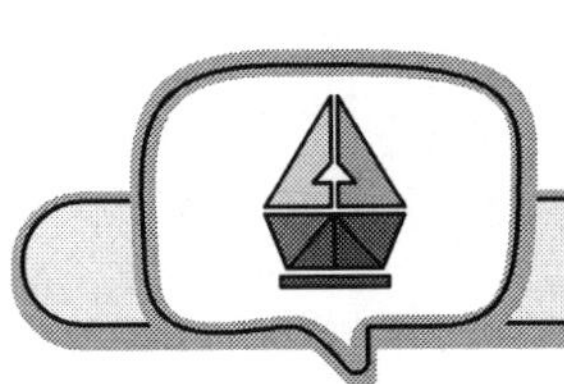

ARMS

CUPS can help make your writing make sense, but ARMS can make your writing more fun to read!

A - add

* Add sentences or words to improve your writing

R - remove

* Remove unneeded or extra words or sentences

M - move

* Move words, sentences, or paragraphs so your writing makes sense

S - substitute

* Substitute words or punctuation.

Let's look at the story you fixed up with CUPS, and see if we can make it even better with ARMS!

Read the original story below.

One sunny day, Lucy and her friend Tommy went to the park. They brought their frisbees and soccer ball, and played for hours. Lucy's mom packed a picnic with sandwiches, fruit, and chips. They ate it under a big oak tree. Lucy said, "I can't believe what a great day we had!"

Now, **read** the story again. The step of ARMS has been done for you. The added words and sentences have been underlined. **How does it impact the story?**

One sunny day, Lucy and her friend Tommy went to <u>Big Oak Park</u>. They brought their frisbees and soccer ball, and played for hours. Lucy's mom packed a delicious picnic with <u>turkey</u> sandwiches, <u>bananas, grapes and BBQ chips</u>. They ate it under a big oak tree. Lucy said, "I can't believe what a great day we had!" <u>Lucy's mom hugged her and said, "I'm glad we spent it together!"</u>

Take a look at a piece of your writing. If you don't have one handy, you can use your friendly letter from Activity 4 in Week 15.

Directions: Read through your writing piece with ARMS. **Write** your new and improved piece below!

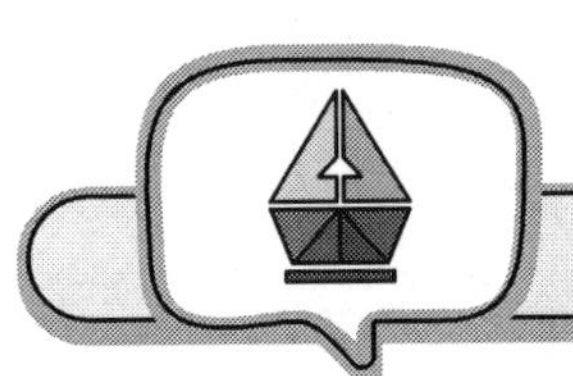

Using Your Charts

In first grade, you probably saw charts like this.

Blends

bl	cl	fl	gl
pl	sl	br	cr
dr	fr	gr	pr
tr	sk	sm	sn

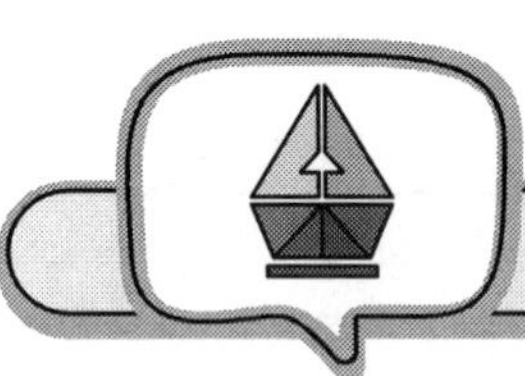

sp	st	sw

sh	ch	th	wh

ai	ay	eigh	au
aw	ui	igh	ea

 Bee	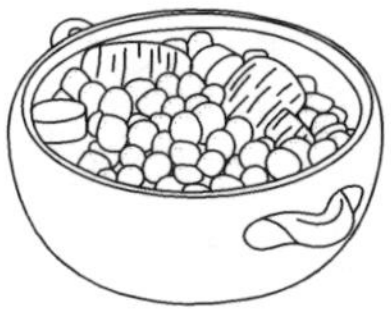 Stew	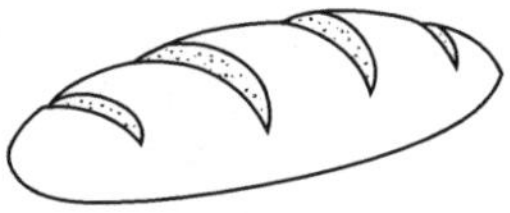 Bread	 Mouth
ee	ew	ea	ou
 Snow	 Boat	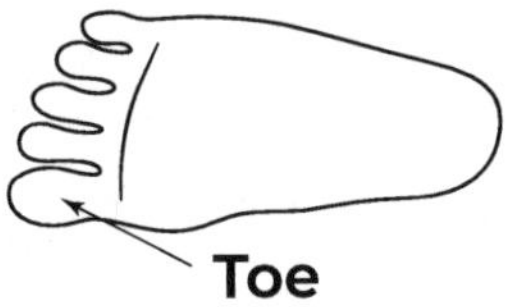 Toe	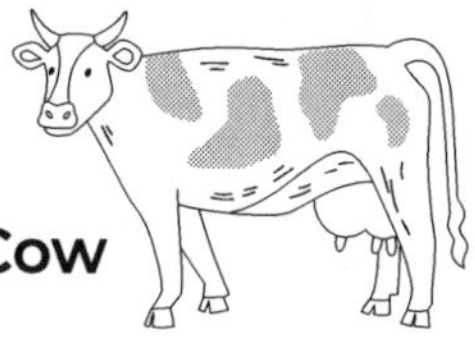 Cow
ow	oa	oe	ow
 Coin	 Boy	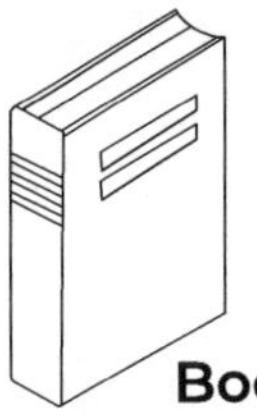 Book	 Moon
oi	oy	oo	oo

Star	Flower	Girl	Fork
ar	er	ir	or

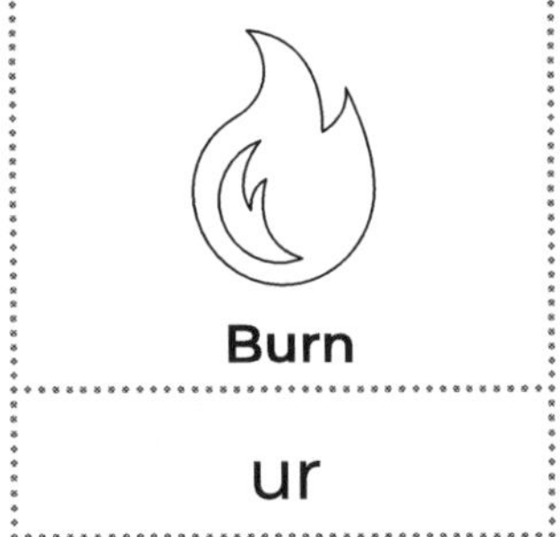

Burn
ur

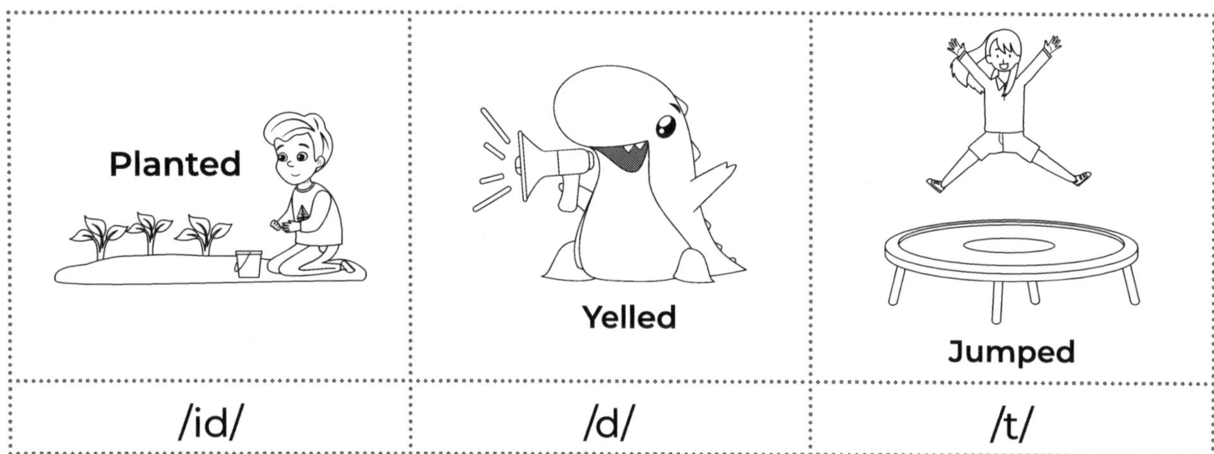

Though these charts were helpful when you were learning how to read words, they are also really helpful when you are spelling words while writing or proofreading!

When you are writing, have charts like this handy to help you out.

Directions: Read the piece of writing below. **Circle** the words that are spelled incorrectly. Then, **rewrite** the incorrect words on the lines. The first one has been completed for you.

Once upon a time, there was a big, scary (jragon) He could blo fire from his mowf. The people in ton hid when they sau him in the sky. Then, one dai, a little gurl wantid to see if the dragon was sad. She asked him if he wanted to be friends with hur. The dragon said yes! Aftur that, no one was scared of the dragon.

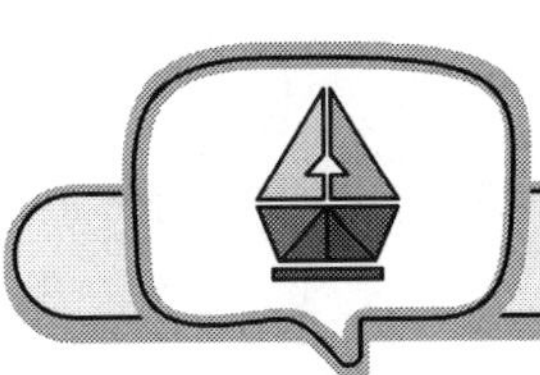

1. Dragon

2.

3.

4.

5.

6.

7.

8.

9.

10.

ARMS, CUPS, and Spelling Strategies - Make it Better!

A lot of people think that the tough work in writing is getting started, but that's not true! You do your best writing work when you go back and make a writing piece the best it can be. Great writers have a saying, "When you think you're done, you've only just begun!

For this activity, you'll write a quick piece of writing. This can be about whatever you want, but a few ideas are below!

* Write about a time something happened to you

* Write a teaching book about an animal

* Write about why something you love is the very best

Then, you'll go through ARMS, CUPS, and your spelling strategies to make your piece even better!

<u>First Draft</u>

Second Draft

Snap Word Practice

Today we will learn **three** new snap words! With your adult, read the snap words below.

great   favorite   maybe

Write the words in the boxes below.

Now let's practice our new words by playing a game called **Timed Write**. You'll play this game once for **each** word.

Directions: Start a timer for one minute. Write your word as **many** times as you can in one minute. Then, see if you can beat your time. If you need more space to write, complete this activity in your notebook.

Word: great

Word: maybe

Word: favorite

Before you go, review your snap words. If you find one you don't know, **circle** it so you know which words you need to practice!

better	follow	happen	different	very
somewhere	anyone	nobody	outside	question
slowly	suddenly	probably	usually	answer
goes	does	begin	trouble	special
great	excited	beautiful	old	when
went	what	where	together	several
begin	before	themselves	either	while
everybody	enough	again	being	ready
sometimes	understand	with	against	terrible
through	excited	everything	about	bare
bear	great	favorite	maybe	

WEEK 20

Review week

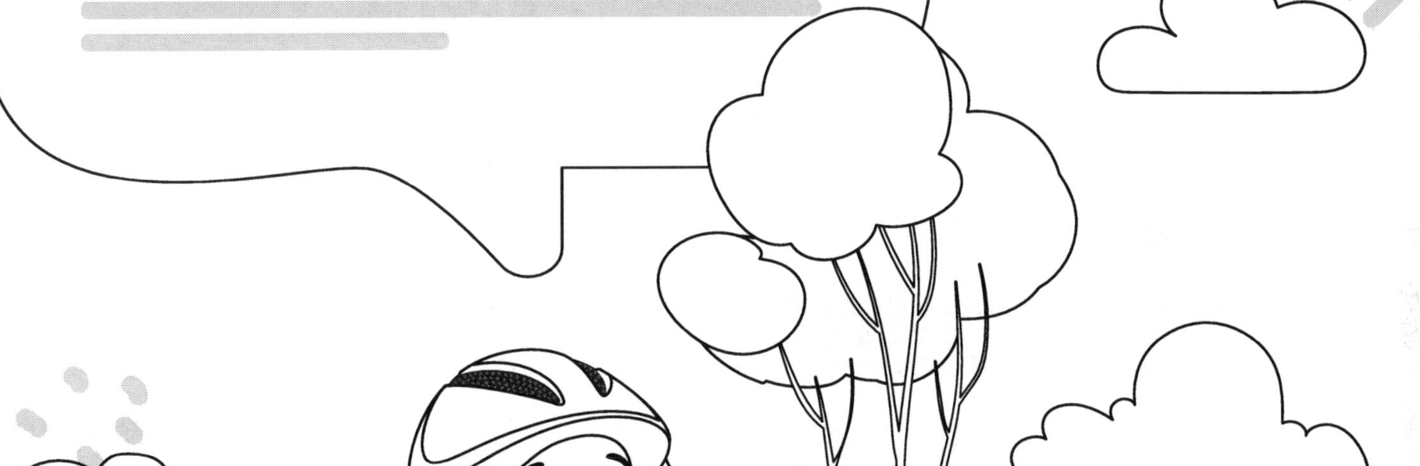

Congratulations! This is your last week of your second grade workbook. This week, you'll review everything you've learned.

You've learned so much over the past few weeks! Let's celebrate your learning this week and review all the great things you've learned to make you a super reader and writer.

Here's a quick summary of what you learned.

* A **homophone** is a word that sounds the same as another word, but it means something different. (Week 3)

* **Contractions** are two words that have been stuck together with an apostrophe. (Week 4)

* You reviewed **common** and **proper nouns**, and you learned that a **possessive noun** uses and apostrophe and an s after a noun to show that an object belongs to a noun. (Week 5)

* A **plural noun** is used to show that there is more than one of something, and you learned some special rules for making nouns plural. (Week 6)

* **Compound words** are two words stuck together. (Week 7)

* A **root word** is a word that has a meaning all by itself. **Prefixes** and **suffixes** are word parts that can be added onto a root word to change what it means. (Week 8)

* **Verb agreement** means that all of the words in a sentence need to work together to make it make sense. (Week 9)

* **Adjectives** describe nouns, and **adverbs** describe verbs. (Week 10)

* An **interrogative** is a question word. When you see an interrogative in a sentence, you should end it with a question mark. (Week 12)

* A **preposition** is a word that is used to tell us more about where, how, or when a noun is doing something. (Week 13)

* A **pronoun** is a word that takes the place of a noun. (Week 14)

* **Commas** are another type of punctuation. They are used in the opening and closings of letters, dates, in lists, and before a conjunction in a compound sentence. (Weeks 15 and 17)

* **Conjunctions** are words that are used to connect two sentences together. (Week 16)

* **Compound sentences** are two simple sentences connected together with a comma and a conjunction. (Week 17)

* **Collective nouns** are nouns used to refer to a group of people, things, or animals. (Week 18)

* You can use many proofreading and spelling strategies, including ARMS, CUPS, checking your snap words, and using the word parts you learned in first grade. (Week 19)

Wow! You've done a lot of hard work this year! Congratulations! In the activities on the next few pages, you'll get a chance to brush up on anything you still need some extra practice on.

Correcting and Comprehending Passages

You'll put all of your learning together in this activity!

Directions: Read the passage below. Check the passage for:

* Homophones

* Contractions

* Plural nouns

* Verb agreement

* Commas

* Capitalization

* Verb agreement

* Punctuation

* Spelling

I went to the park with my friendies? We played on the swinges, and the slide. It was so mush fun! I eated a yummy Ice Cream coan and we laughs a lot I cant wait to go two the park again.

Rewrite the passage correctly.

....

....

....

....

....

Answer the questions below about the passage.

1. Where did the person go with their friends?

   A. The park

   B. The zoo

   C. The school playground

2. What did the person eat?

   A. Hotdogs

   B. Hamburgers

   C. Ice cream

3. What did the person and their friends play on?

   A. The monkey bars

   B. The slide

   C. The merry-go-round

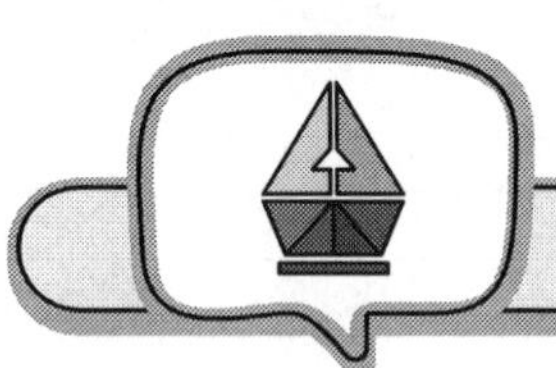

Nouns, Adjectives, and Adverbs

Directions: Read each sentence carefully. Find and underline the nouns, circle the adjectives, and draw a box around the adverbs. The first one has been done for you.Not all sentences will have all three kinds of words.

1. The (happy) <u>dog</u> runs quickly.

2. There are colorful flowers in the garden.

3. My little sister sings beautifully.

4. The noisy wind blew gently.

5. The fast car races loudly around the track.

6. The tall giraffe eats slowly.

7. The knight bravely rescued the lonely princess.

8. The hungry cat meowed loudly for food.

9. The shiny stars twinkle brightly in the night sky.

10. The curious squirrel climbs the tree carefully.

Now, **write** a sentence of your own. Underline the noun, circle the adjective, and draw a box around the adverb in your sentence.

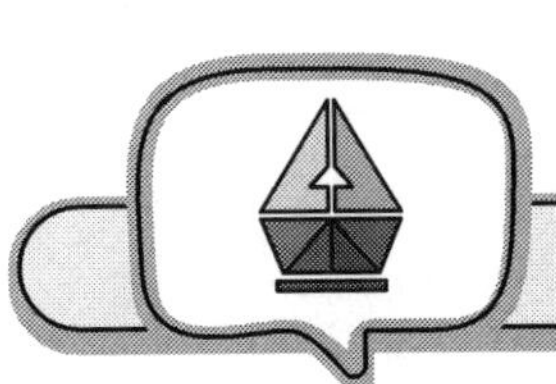

Collective Nouns and Compound Sentences

Directions: Combine the two simple sentences into a compound sentence. **Underline** the collective noun in each sentence. **Circle** the conjunction.

Example:

The sun is shining.	The flock of birds are singing.

The sun is shining, (and) the <u>flock</u> of birds are singing.

Ollie has a whole collection of books.	She loves to read.

My class wanted to play outside.	It was raining.

We went to the zoo.	We saw a pride of lions.

The flowers are blooming.	The swarm of bees is buzzing.

The pack of dogs is howling.	My cat is upset.

Write your own compound sentence with a collective noun!

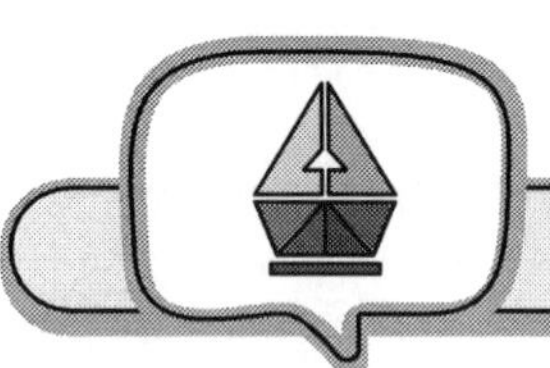

Interrogative Prepositions

Directions: Underline the interrogative word and circle the preposition.

1. Why did the cat hide in the closet?

2. How are you feeling on this sunny day?

3. What is your favorite game at the park?

4. When is your birthday party with all your friends?

5. Why do birds fly over the trees?

6. Where does the bus stop on your street?

7. How do you make a cake without eggs?

8. What do you want from the restaurant?

9. Why is the school concert in the evening?

10. When did you laugh during the funny movie?

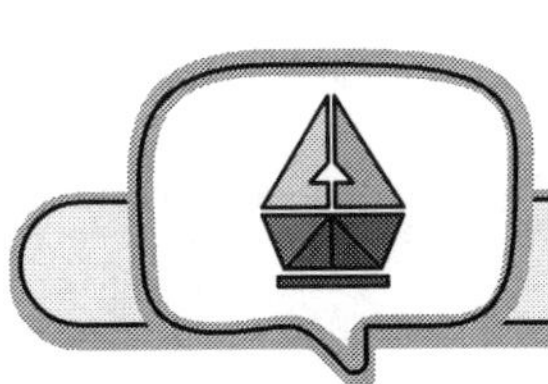

Write your own sentences with interrogatives or prepositions. For an extra challenge, see if you can write some sentences with both!

1. ____

2. ____

3. ____

4. ____

5. ____

Spelling Test

In this activity, you will take a quick spelling test.

Directions: Find an adult or a friend to read fifteen of your sight words to you, one word at a time. They can pick any of the words you've learned this year.

When they call out a word, you'll write it on the line. At the end, work together to see how you did.

1. ______________________________

2. ______________________________

3. ______________________________

4. ______________________________

5. ______________________________

6. ______________________________

7. ______________________________

8. ______________________________

9. ______________________________

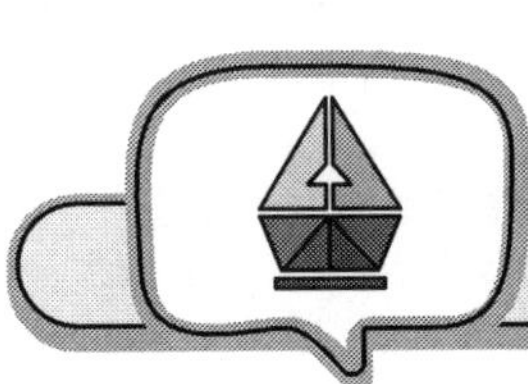

10. ____

11. ____

12. ____

13. ____

14. ____

15. ____

Word Flash Cards

You've worked hard all year to learn your snap words, but there were a lot of snap words. You'll need your snap words in third grade, so today, you'll make yourself some flash cards to help you remember the words you're still having trouble with.

Directions: Read all of your second grade snap words. If you come to a word you don't know, **circle** it.

Then, make flash cards of each word. Practice them everyday until you know them all!

eight	ate	see	sea	eye
I	hear	here	two	too
to	your	you're	there	their
they're	school	people	cousin	was
better	follow	happen	different	very
somewhere	anyone	nobody	outside	question
slowly	suddenly	probably	usually	answer
goes	does	begin	trouble	special
great	excited	beautiful	old	when
went	what	where	together	several
begin	before	themselves	either	while
everybody	enough	again	being	ready
sometimes	understand	with	against	terrible
through	excited	everything	about	bare
bear	great	favorite	maybe	could

Answer Sheets

To see the answer key to the entire workbook, you can easily download the answer key from our website!

*Due to the high request from parents and teachers, we have removed the answer key from the workbook so you do not need to rip out the answer key while students work on the workbook.

 To watch free video explanations go to: **argoprep.com/spelling2** OR scan the QR Code: 

Place your mouse over the workbook you have, and you will see the "Download Answers" button.

For detailed video instructions on how to access the "Answer Sheets," please scan this QR code. 

Books explanations

2nd Grade Common Core Math: Spanish Edition

2nd Grade Introducing Math & Science Workbook

2nd Grade Science: Daily Practice Workbook | 20 Weeks of Fun...

2nd Grade Social Studies: Daily Practice Workbook

Kids Winter Academy by ArgoPrep: Grade 2

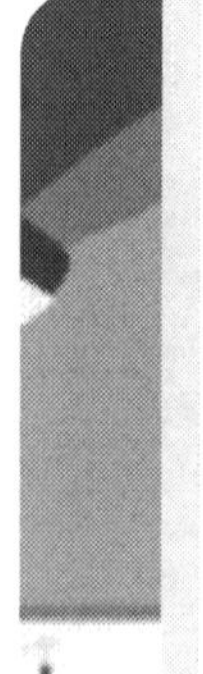
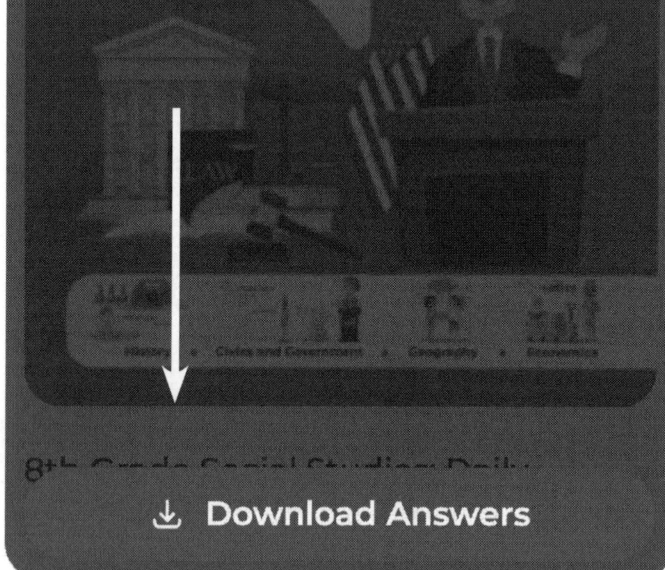

4th Grade Social Studies: Practice Workbook

Made in the USA
Columbia, SC
26 August 2024